The
Steve Young
Story

Laury Livsey

PRIMA PUBLISHING

*To Monica, who encouraged me every step of
the way, and to SAN and Mike A.
Two better friends I know not.*

PRIMA PUBLISHING and colophon are trademarks of Prima Communications, Inc.

Library of Congress Cataloging-in-Publication Data

Livsey, Laury.
   The Steve Young story / Laury Livsey.
      p. cm.
   Includes index.
   ISBN 0-7615-0194-0
   ISBN 0-7615-0766-6 (pbk.)
     1. Young, Steve, 1961–. 2. Football players—United States—Biography. 3. San Francisco 49ers (Football team) I. Title.
GV939.Y69L58   1995
796.332'092 B—dc20   95-31504
                                                        CIP

96 97 98 99 00 01 AA 10 9 8 7 6 5 4 3 2 1

Printed in the United States of America

How to Order
Single copies may be ordered from Prima Publishing, P.O. Box 1260BK, Rocklin, CA 95677; telephone (916) 632-4400. Quantity discounts are also available. On your letterhead, include information concerning the intended use of the books and the number of books you wish to purchase.

Contents

CONTENTS

CHAPTER ONE

An Imposing Barrier

Steve Young negotiated the turns of El Monte Road as he drove the wooded streets near his home in Los Altos Hills, California. He was coming from the airport after a short trip to Irving, Texas. It was a visit that hadn't gone particularly well. For the second consecutive year the San Francisco 49er quarterback was going home two victories short of his goal. His 1993 season, just like the 1992 one, had ended two weeks too early. The Dallas Cowboys, not the San Francisco 49ers, would represent the National Football Conference in the Super Bowl. Young would have to watch the National Football League's preeminent game on TV if he bothered switching it on at all.

As he drove, Young's thoughts were on one thing and one thing only—the loss.

Four hours earlier, he'd done what he could against the Cowboys. But the San Francisco defense could not stop Dallas's offense, and no matter what Young did, it wasn't good enough.

He thought about the Cowboys, how they were a better team than the 49ers, and how his team was slipping. The 49er fans would feel the same way. Only they'd single out one player to blame for the two playoff failures and that somebody was him. It would be a nasty next couple of days. Young was certain of that. He had been around long enough to know what he was in for. Monday's sports sections all over the country would question his ability to lead a team. It would be a tired old storyline. The columnists would call him a good quarterback with great statistics, essentially a quarterback who didn't have the ability to lead a team to a championship. In other words, he was no Joe Montana. Or Troy Aikman, for that matter. The talk shows would take their turns too. Young could turn on KNBR radio in San Francisco and listen to callers blister him. Frank from Sausalito, Mary from San Ramon, and Dick from Benicia would all basically say the same thing: Young ain't no Joe. "How many times did Joe take the Niners to the Super Bowl?" they'd ask. Of course, the answer would be the same every time—four more than Steve Young.

It was the same thing Danny White heard while he was playing quarterback for the Dallas Cowboys. White, a superb athlete who had a phenomenal grasp of the Cowboy offense, never played in a Super Bowl. The Cowboys were always on the cusp, losing three straight NFC championship games from 1980 to 1982. White followed Roger Staubach, the beloved quarterback icon of Cowboy lore. No matter what White did, he could never measure up to the Staubach legend. After consecutive championship game losses, Young's script had begun to resemble White's. In this new scenario, instead of White-Staubach, it was Young-Montana. To the football cognoscenti, Steve Young was becoming the 1990s version of Danny White.

It had been five years since the Vince Lombardi Trophy, exemplifying a Super Bowl title, had parked itself in the 49ers' trophy case. The fans were getting impatient, especially with Young. The deified Montana had been traded to the Kansas City Chiefs just so Young could have his turn. Given this opportunity, Young had fumbled away his chance not once, but twice. For Steve Young to replace Saint Joe and not win a Super Bowl was bad enough. To not even get the Niners out of the league championship game was heresy of the highest order.

It was all stuff Young had heard before. Still, it didn't make listening to the irrational spleen-venting of Niner fans or the brutal newspaper columns and talk show diatribes any easier to take.

Young would have to live with the criticism, but he was fully aware where the problem really lay. It all came down to Charles Haley. Dallas had Charles Haley and San Francisco didn't. The Niners had practically given Haley away in a trade before the 1992 season, and now the quick, strong defensive end was making Young's life miserable. Not only was he chasing Young all over the field, he *wasn't* bearing down on Dallas quarterback Troy Aikman. Haley was a huge addition for the Cowboys and Young knew it. He hoped Aikman appreciated his good fortune.

As the second loss sank in, Young began to realize he would never quarterback the 49ers in the Super Bowl unless some drastic changes were made on the defensive side of the ball. Even the Man himself, former 49er coach Bill Walsh, the man credited with designing the San Francisco offense, once said, "A pass rush late in the game is the key to NFL football." After watching Young run for his life against the Cowboys, who could argue?

Young wasn't sure what plans the team had for the future, he just knew where it stood on January 16, 1994. Dallas had scored 38 points to the Niners 21. It was a 17-point loss that, in reality, wasn't even that close. The simple fact was the 49ers desperately needed better defensive players. Even 49er owner Edward DeBartolo Jr. concurred as he stewed on the plane ride back to California. He'd told reporters after the game that San Francisco's failure to stop Dallas was the reason for the loss. "We have to get better," he said. It was a must. Young could post all sorts of gaudy numbers, but if the team allowed opponents' offenses to score in the 30s, it was a lost cause. Young understood this better than anybody. He just hoped DeBartolo's talk about improving the defense wasn't just Eddie D. blowing smoke.

It had been a long season, a long two years, really, and Young was tired of feeling like he was fighting a losing battle. As he turned onto Stonebrook Avenue toward his home, Young was glad, in a way, that the season was over.

CHAPTER TWO

Salt Lake City, Utah

Dorene Tester still remembers Sherry Young ringing the bell of her home on Lone Peak Drive in the Cottonwood area of Salt Lake City. It was the summer of 1967.

"You've got to come and see what these boys have done," Mrs. Young said with both an exasperated and amused tone to her voice. Dorene Tester dropped what she was doing and walked next door to the Youngs' house at 1541 Lone Peak Drive. As Mrs. Young escorted her neighbor into the kitchen, they both began laughing. There stood three boys in front of the sink, oblivious to anything going on around them. They had more important things to concentrate on. They had gotten into the cupboard and taken cocoa, sugar, salt, flour, pepper—you name it—and were mixing it with water to form some sort of concoction in a glass. The sink was a mess, with ingredients scattered everywhere. Since it was the Young house, both women knew who the ringleader was. All Steve Young could do was turn and look at his mom. The six-year-old boy was busted.

"You try to look back but you really don't pay that much attention to one individual child in a neighborhood, but I remember Steve was a very handsome young man all through his growing up. He had that dark curly hair, and that infectious smile," says Tester.

The hair is still curly, and the smile is as infectious as ever. Otherwise, things haven't exactly stayed the same for Steve Young.

• • •

LeGrande Young met Sherry Steed while they were both students at Brigham Young University in Provo, Utah. He was fresh off a Mormon mission to Australia, was majoring in political science, and had designs on attending law school. She was a coed from Las Cruces, New Mexico. LeGrande was also a pretty decent football player on a pretty crummy team. The BYU Cougars during LeGrande's senior year finished with a 3-7 mark, which was about normal for BYU. The Cougars' claim to fame that season was that they led the nation in punting average. That pretty much told the story of BYU football. During his senior year of 1959, LeGrande was the Cougars' rushing leader, gaining 423 yards. But he could not crack the Skyline Conference all-league team that featured two future pro football hall of famers, Larry Wilson of Utah and Utah State's Merlin Olsen.

LeGrande, nicknamed Grit, eventually married Sherry, and when his college eligibility ended and he graduated from BYU, it was off to law school at the University of Utah, 45 miles north of Provo in Salt Lake City. The couple lived in a married student housing complex known as Stadium Village. Their one-bedroom wooden-floored, wooden-walled apartment had previously been a military barracks, and was pretty spartan. There weren't a lot of luxuries while Grit was in law school.

The University of Utah was initially called the University of Deseret when it was founded on February 28, 1850, at the behest of a man named Brigham Young, who just so happened to be LeGrande Young's great-great grandfather. It was the same Brigham Young who had a university in Provo named for him too.

Brigham Young, colonizer, territorial governor, and successor to Joseph Smith as president of The Church of Jesus Christ of Latter-day Saints, was also a practicing polygamist. During his lifetime, Brigham Young had 55 wives, including Emily Dow Partridge Young, who was wife number eight. All told, 16 of the 55 wives bore him 57 children. In turn, those children had children, and the children's children had children. And 74 years after Brigham Young's death in 1877, his most famous offspring was born.

At the University of Utah, Grit was entrenched in his studies, and Sherry took classes at the U., from March of 1961 until August, when her burden became too heavy, both literally and figuratively. Sherry was pregnant.

On October 11, 1961, 10 girls and 14 boys were born in Salt Lake City–area hospitals. One of the boys was Brigham's great-great-great grandson, the first child of LeGrande and Sherry. They named their son Jon Steven Young.

When Grit Young graduated from law school in 1964, he and Sherry bought their first home on Lone Peak Drive, a relatively new, middle-class neighborhood in a southeastern section of Salt Lake City. The Youngs lived among a variety of neighbors. There was a bank vice president, a glass salesman, a brick mason, a territory manager for a spark plug company, a draftsman, and Grit, an attorney for the Anaconda Corporation, a mining concern located on the west side of Salt Lake City.

Grit and Sherry were active members of their Mormon ward, and quickly became friends with most of their neighbors. They were settling into their professional life together. Two years to the day after Steve's birth, Mike, who would become Steve's playmate, was born, making the Youngs a four-person family.

It didn't take long for Steve and Mike to make friends with the other kids on Lone Peak Drive. They all attended Meadow Moor Elementary, with afterschool and summers consumed by games of tag, dubbed Game Tag by the Lone Peak youth. The Young house was also a gathering place for kids, and it was made even more user-friendly when Grit nailed up a basketball hoop in the backyard. Attached at only six feet, the hoop was an attractive addition to the neighborhood. However it was the Youngs' front yard that really held sway.

"They had a pretty good front yard, and the people who lived next door to them didn't have a fence," says Rocky Smith, who grew up across the street from the Youngs. Smith, five years older than Steve, usually organized the football games on the spacious Young front yard and the Tester yard next door. Smith would enlist Chris Kristic, who lived two houses down from the Youngs, the Perkins brothers, Bryce, Mark, and Keith, and Steve Young for some tackle football games, using a real, leather football. There was plenty of room for the boys to play, especially when Grit's 1965 Oldsmobile Dynamic wasn't parked in the driveway.

"Steve was pretty good. He was younger than all of us, but he was still pretty good. We were bigger, but he wanted to play. He insisted on playing," Smith says. "Every once in a while he'd get a little hurt and he'd cry. We'd have to quiet him up, you know, because he was so much younger. His mom would come out and just have a fit. She'd be mad at us, but he would just get up and shake it off. He was a real tough little kid. He was one of the toughest little kids in the neighborhood. In fact, when we played he used to run into the biggest kids around. That's the way he played football even when he was that young."

Steve would play tackle football with kids much older than him and take them all on, but he was afraid to go to school without his mother. That was the dichotomy of Steve Young. He was basically a shy kid who was embarrassed by his looks; a kid who would wear a ski cap to school to make his hair straighter because he thought his curly hair somehow made him weird. Socially he struggled. Athletically, he flourished.

Young playing football is the one lasting memory of Christy Sturgeon, a neighbor from down the street who frequently babysat Steve and Mike. "They were really good kids. I just remember when Steve was little he played football with his brother," says Sturgeon. "That was their thing."

The Youngs' stay on Lone Peak Drive was a relatively short one. In 1969, the Anaconda Corporation transferred Grit Young to its New York office. The Youngs sold their house, piled into the Oldsmobile, and bid farewell to Utah. It was a sad parting for all concerned. It was in Utah where Grit and Sherry had met and been educated, where Steve, Mike, and later the third and fourth Young children, Melissa and Tom, were born. For Steve, it was goodbye to the football games in the front yard.

CHAPTER THREE

The Move East

When you're a family, especially a Mormon family, transferred to New York from Salt Lake City, the last place you want to live is New York City. You want the suburbs. You want little league, and tree-lined streets. You want a house, not a high-rise apartment. Those were LeGrande and Sherry Young's sentiments when they began house hunting after word came that Anaconda was transferring LeGrande to the east coast. There were plenty of places to turn, but they chose a house in the Riverside neighborhood of Greenwich, Connecticut. If they wanted the suburbs, they got it in Greenwich.

The first four houses built on a new street named Split Timber Place, by North Mianus Elementary School, numbered one through four. The Engels, the Pryors, the Moores, and the Wallenbergers owned those houses. Slowly, the neighborhood grew as new houses began springing up, including the two-story job with the wood-shingled facade at 27 Split Timber Place that became the Youngs' permanent home in 1970. The neighbors on one side were the Wards. The Morells lived on the other. Almost all the couples on the street were divided along the same lines. The men worked in New York City and the women stayed home with the kids. In the early '70s, the residents living on Split Timber Place were similar to the people who had bought homes on Lone Peak Drive in Salt Lake City—mostly younger families with husbands/fathers who worked nine-to-five for a living.

Down the road a bit was an entirely different setting. Back Country Greenwich, as locals referred to this exclusive area, was nothing like Riverside. Although the Youngs were doing well financially, and LeGrande had carved out a niche as a labor lawyer, they didn't ask their realtor to look for any houses on Sound Beach Avenue. The four- and five-acre mansions set away from the streets housed people like Joseph Levine, the movie mogul; Tom Seaver, the New York Mets' pitcher; and Roy Cohn, the attorney and Senator Joseph McCarthy protege. That was the Beverly Hills of Connecticut. The curiosity seekers who made their way to Greenwich would drive past the estates on Lake Avenue or Round Hill Road hoping to catch a glimpse of one of Greenwich's many celebrities. Split Timber Place held no such allure. Compared to the national average, the Youngs' house was in an affluent area. In Greenwich terms, their neighborhood was strictly middle-class.

When the Youngs moved to Greenwich, Dorothy Hamill, a young figure skater a few years older than Steve, lived with her family on 172 Riverside Avenue in the city's "low-rent district." She would be the biggest thing to come out of this town until a certain quarterback came along.

• • •

Young quickly fit into his new surroundings when he discovered that sports were the thing in Greenwich. At North Mianus Elementary School, his recesses were spent with some type of ball, and he usually wrote his school reports about National Football League quarterbacks. It was what he knew. He'd always enjoyed reading, and as he began reading regularly, he would always gravitate to the books about football players written for grade-school readers. Reading and football players became the particular passions in his life. In Young's bedroom, posters of Roger Staubach, the Dallas Cowboys' quarterback, adorned his walls. A's adorned his report cards. Sports and school came naturally to Young.

As he got older, he became more serious about sports and how he competed in them. Although he had fun catching the Metro-North to New York City to watch the Rangers or the Knicks play, it was more fun to play the sports, mainly because he was very good in whatever he tried. Another selling point was the games themselves. They were becoming a little more sophisticated and a lot more organized than the ones he played on his front lawn in Salt Lake City.

Grit Young recognized early that all of his sons were going to compete in sports and do well. He particularly noticed his oldest son's amazing coordination, and his ability to do things at a very young age that his peers couldn't. Steve's ability to dribble a basketball as a three-year-old amazed Grit. He wasn't predicting anything special for his son, but it was not surprising to Grit when Steve excelled on the football field, the basketball court, and the baseball diamond.

It was at North Mianus where Young got his first taste of organized football, playing for the North Mianus Cowboys of the Greenwich Midget League. In his first year at North Mianus, Young, for the only time in his life, didn't play quarterback. That position was reserved for Dave Grimsich, who was two years older than Young and more developed at the time. Ironically, Grimsich and Young would follow similar paths. Both their fathers had played college football—Dan Grimsich for the University of Illinois and Grit for BYU. The younger Grimsich eventually went to Boston College to play QB before finishing his career at Rhode Island. So for Steve Young, there was no shame in playing behind a talented guy like Grimsich. Young played running back, which was okay, too, because it was a position that allowed Young to do what he did best—run. He even got to pass a little. A pet play for the Cowboys was a halfback pass, with Young the trigger man. North Mianus would send Bill Valle on a pass pattern, and as the defense converged on Young, he would spot Valle, usually all by himself. "Every time we used that play it seemed like we would score," says Peter Duncan, a fullback who played alongside Young on those teams.

After elementary school, Young moved on to Eastern Junior High, one of three junior highs in the city that fed into Greenwich High School. In his seventh-grade year at Eastern in 1974, Young's team won every game. As an eighth-grader, Eastern ran the board again. That season, in their six games the Gators were a juggernaut, outscoring their opponents 245-24. By this time, Young was the Gators' quarterback, but he wasn't the team's star. Ninth-graders Bob Whitely and Herb Foote scored 16 and 10 touchdowns respectively. Young, who wore the uniform number eight for the first time, became adept at handing the ball off and watching Whitely and Foote do their things. Whitely was the fullback, a big runner who could bull for yardage, while Foote, who everybody called Herbie, was quicker and more compact. Young wouldn't throw very often because the running game was so potent, and because he wasn't very accurate when he did put the ball up.

"Eastern was very good, and Steve was just a great runner. It didn't look like he was running that fast, but it seemed like you could never tackle him," says Frank Parelli, who attended Western Junior High and played against Young before becoming Young's teammate at Greenwich. "He'd give you a little move and then he'd run 60 yards, 70 yards, whatever it was, for a touchdown. He was a year behind us, and everybody was pretty impressed because he wasn't that big but he was just such a great runner."

Many of the guys from those Eastern teams would go on to play with Young at Greenwich High.

One of the rules established by coach Mike Ornato at Greenwich High School, when he took over as head football coach in 1972, was that sophomores could not play on the Cardinals' varsity team. There would be no exceptions. It didn't matter how good you were, who your older brother was, who your parents were, or what your pedigree was in junior high. At Greenwich High, if you were an underclassman you played junior varsity ball.

Apparently Ornato's method worked. In his first six seasons guiding the Cardinals' football fortunes, the team had posted a 35-8-2 record. The success Ornato had with the Cardinals didn't come as a surprise to the locals in and around Greenwich. Winning football games had become an expected part of the autumn season long before Ornato got there. Sam Rutigliano was an early Greenwich coach who made a name for himself before taking his coaching acumen first to the University of Connecticut then to the NFL where he was the Cleveland Browns' head coach.

When Ornato was handed Greenwich's coaching reins, his charge was to uphold the Cardinals' strong football tradition. Ornato did that by never experiencing a losing season as Greenwich's coach. He always seemed to have an abundance of talent from which to draw, sending many of his players to four-year colleges on football scholarships. Eastern Junior High had a reputation for producing a lot of skill-position guys. Central seemed to be a breeding ground for defensive players, and Western, located in the poorest part of Greenwich, didn't have a well-defined reputation. Yet all three schools were well-represented with players on any given Greenwich High roster.

Since Greenwich High was a three-year high school, skilled players only had to play JV one year before joining the varsity club. That was Steve Young's plan. He would cut his teeth on JV ball for one year before moving on to the big time.

When Ornato looked at the 1977 Greenwich junior varsity team, the players who would make up the bulk of the talent on the 1978 and '79 teams, his streak of winning seasons appeared to be in jeopardy. For a group of players that hadn't been accustomed to losing in little league or in junior high play, that season came as a huge shock—especially to Young, the team's starting quarterback. To put it bluntly, the 1977 Greenwich High junior varsity team was horrendous.

"They were not a good unit in 10th grade," says Ron Fischetti, who was in Young's class and covered football for both *The Beak*, Greenwich High's student newspaper, and for the *Greenwich Time*. "They were not a very large team physically, and they got run over a lot."

"We were pretty horrible. One of the worst ever," says Greg Campbell, a wide receiver who took two years off from football in junior high and then returned for that ill-fated JV season.

The team won only one game in that 1977 season, and it was anybody's guess how the players would respond when they moved to the varsity level. Young's natural leadership skills showed through during that dismal season, and he was elected captain of the junior varsity team. He would make it a JV captain trifecta, serving as captain of the basketball and baseball teams too.

By the time Young was 16, a lot of things were going on in his life. He had passed what is considered the first rite of passage for any kid when he got his driver's license. With that achievement came a semi-inheritance from Young's father—Grit's 1965 navy blue Oldsmobile Dynamic. With a ride of his own, Young promptly decorated it to his liking by putting a bunch of Greenwich High football helmet decals on it. He'd christened the car "The Cardinal." As far as Young's friends were concerned, he should have turned his father down when his dad offered him the car.

"It was kind of a car, if that's what you want to call it. It was something. I was amazed that it moved sometimes," says Willie Atkins, a teammate of Young's on the Greenwich High basketball team. Atkins drove a station wagon—pretty worn out in its own right—that his parents bequeathed to him. It was nicer than The Cardinal, but

Atkins didn't have a whole lot of room to talk. What the cars did do was serve their purposes well. Atkins's got him to basketball practice. The Cardinal did the same for Young.

"We loved sports," Atkins adds. "We played constantly." When it was basketball season, Young and his buddies Ed Sheehan, Jim Gannon, Steve Gebhardt, and Atkins would play indoors at the Greenwich High gymnasium, or outdoors at North Mianus. They all lived in or near the Riverside area, so everybody was close. When basketball season ended, it was time for baseball.

Says Atkins, "We hung out a lot during the basketball season. Then, when Steven was playing baseball and football he was pretty much hanging out with those crowds. Steven was the type of guy who had friends in all different areas."

"The thing about him is he was very unaffected. He was able to sit down at a table full of guys and whether they played varsity sports or not, he kind of fit in. He was the kind of guy whom everybody liked. It sounds really trite but it's the truth," says Fischetti.

Despite all the time spent with sports, Young's school work was never neglected. He took a lot of advanced classes, spoke French moderately well, and his teachers liked him.

"Steven was very, very serious about school. If he wasn't playing sports or doing something with his church, Steven was doing something educational," says Atkins.

Fischetti continues, "He was not your typical high school athlete in the sense that he did not need a lot of direction. He used to go straight from football to basketball season, and he'd usually miss at least two weeks of practice. And he would step right in."

For Young's first year of varsity football, a major change occurred. Opponents had come to expect the power-I formation from Mike Ornato-coached teams competing in the Fairfield County Interscholastic Athletic Conference. Ornato stayed with the I until the 1978 season when he decided to try something new. The change would be a drastic one.

Attrition is a factor in any high school program. For a three-year high school that doesn't play sophomores, it can be an even tougher problem. Graduation of key players from the 1977 Greenwich team that finished with a 7-1-1 record had decimated the Cardinals' personnel, leaving Ornato with a bunch of first-year varsity players as the core of the '78 club. These were the untested juniors who won one JV game their entire sophomore season—the team with Steve Young as their leader.

With those circumstances in mind, Ornato decided to scrap the I in favor of the wishbone, the offense that called for three running backs in the backfield and a quarterback who, with numerous options, would make things happen. It looked like a good fit, especially for Young. Ornato needed a quarterback who had the intelligence and the athletic ability to run a complicated offense and he had that in Young. Another quarterback, Bill Barber, also had those traits.

Like anybody playing varsity for the first time, Young had high hopes of being named the starter. He had his eye on the Cardinals' quarterback job. The truth was, he had understudy written all over him. Barber, a senior and one of the few players with game experience returning from the 1977 squad, looked like a solid candidate to win the quarterback spot. Ornato had even said so. The real battle for Young seemed to be between he and John Coyle for the right to back up Barber. Young wasn't buying into that scenario. Standing on the sidelines signaling in plays was not the goal to which Young aspired. Young fully expected to beat out Barber and hold off Coyle for the job. Barber had patiently waited for Dave Grimsich to move on so he could have his turn. Both wanted to be Greenwich's number-one quarterback, and even though Young knew he would probably start once Barber graduated, that wasn't good enough. He wanted to be the Greenwich Cardinals' quarterback for two years.

It turned out that the competition for quarterback was not even open. Barber was a big guy, 6-feet-3, with a good arm, and Ornato was counting on him to make the transition to the wishbone. The coach would eventually have to scrap those plans. Just prior to the team's season-opener, Barber went down with a shoulder injury that would force him to miss at least the first three games. That was just enough time for Young to lay claim to the QB job he—the Ten Commandments be damned—coveted.

Ornato had to admit that Young fit the mold of a wishbone quarterback. He was smart, and had picked up the offense pretty quickly. He was fast, and most importantly he had two years to play.

On September 16, 1978, Steve Young trotted onto the Ridgefield High School field as Greenwich's starting quarterback and took apart the Tigers throughout a systematic 27-0 win. Young scored on a quarterback keeper from 10 yards out in the second quarter, and completed 7 of 9 passes for 65 yards in the victory. Young's performance earned him Greenwich High player-of-the-week honors in a vote by his coaches and teammates. It was a great beginning. The following week, Young rushed for 94 yards and threw one touchdown pass in the Cardinals' 20-8 win against Norwalk. The season's first two weeks had been memorable for the junior QB. Young was earning accolades not only for leading Greenwich to the quick start, but also for the seemingly effortless way he operated the wishbone. Young's ability to quickly read defensive keys made him a great decision-maker, and a nightmare for opposing defenses.

"At that point in his career, he hadn't really developed his throwing arm but he was still an absolutely fabulous runner," says Campbell, the wide receiver who didn't see the ball as much as he would have liked. But he understood. "Steve was running quarterback sneaks off our own goal line and running them for big gains."

Young would see the linebackers closing a hole so he'd pitch to the tailback. When the cornerbacks would play too far outside the hash marks in hopes of shutting down the pitchout, Young would turn upfield and keep the ball himself, outrunning any and all comers. That was a particularly effective play for Young, whose superior speed often left defensive backs looking at his cardinal number 14 from behind. Young was making it look easy. Maybe too easy.

On September 30 against Brien McMahon High, Young had a crash-and-burn day to forget. In a 25-0 loss to the league-leading Senators, the Cardinals were held to 48 yards of total offense. Young was 2 of 12 in the passing department, totaling only 17 yards. The 12 attempts were the most he attempted in any one game that season. To compound matters, he could never get the running game going. Barber replaced Young toward the end of the blowout. It was Young's first varsity loss and he wasn't happy about it. He'd done enough losing the year before to last a lifetime.

As he watched the final seconds tick off the clock, Young wondered if the healthy Barber was back in the quarterback picture. Would Barber start the next week's game? Would the quarterbacks platoon? Ornato put an end to any speculation when he announced Young as the next game's starter. As it turned out, the loss to Brien McMahon was Young's only bad outing of the season. His passing was spotty all year, but in an offense geared around the run, Young was accurate enough to occasionally pull a surprise on a defense. He completed only 14 of his 30 passes the remainder of the season, which hardly mattered because Greenwich was winning. What Young wasn't accomplishing via the air he was doing on the ground. He had a 202-yard rushing afternoon against Trumbull High, with his 76- and 72-yard touchdown runs serving as the game's highlights. Young also had 102- and 133-yard rushing games during the Cardinals' 7-2 season. Prior to the Cardinals' final game of the year against Stamford, one of the Black Knights' defensive backs, Doug Brown, called his cousin, Willie Atkins, and told him he was going to nail Young so hard it would knock the quarterback from the game.

"You better warn your buddy," Brown said.

Atkins, Young's teammate on the basketball court, just laughed.

"I'm going to put him out of the game," Brown said.

"You've got to catch him first," Atkins told his cousin.

Atkins' observation was fairly astute. In the first quarter, with Greenwich at Stamford's 35, Young dropped back to pass, pumped once, and then took off running. Nobody touched him as he walked into the end zone. In the fourth quarter, it was the same thing, only from 39 yards out. Atkins couldn't help but smile as he watched the game from the stands of Boyle Stadium.

"On that second run, he went right toward my cousin and put some sort of a move on him. I don't remember exactly what it was but I ended up laughing because my cousin never laid a finger on him. To this day, I have conversations with my cousin and we laugh and joke about it."

It was a good year, and Young earned a spot on the *Bridgeport Post* All-AA Division second team behind St. Joseph's quarterback Bill Meade. The Cardinals, however, didn't make the playoffs.

In high school, Young understood that if he was going to become a well-rounded quarterback, he couldn't always rely on his feet to get the job done. He recognized his shortcomings as a passer, and he took steps to improve. Every Friday night at the conclusion of practice, after the rest of the team had gone over to the gym to eat treats made by the cheerleaders, Young and wide receiver Frank Parelli would stick around and work on routes, timing, and, of course, passing and catching.

"I'd just run patterns and he'd throw me the ball," says Parelli. "He was a hard worker and maybe he thought his passing was a little weakness and he wanted to better himself. It helped us to work together. I always thought he had a real good arm; it was just a matter of throwing the ball more. As a team we just didn't throw that much."

Steve Young's development as a passer was still in the early stages. But his reputation as a runner was firmly solidified, as was the recognition he was enjoying as one of Greenwich High School's top athletes—if not the top athlete. He was the all-American boy. He was a top-notch student, athletics seemed to come easy for him, he was blessed with good looks, and he had an ability to make everybody feel comfortable. It was no surprise in high school when Young began dating Christy Fichtner, who just happened to be, by all accounts, the best-looking girl in school. She was also a cheerleader, and was homecoming queen her senior year. Like Young, she would go on to accomplish quite a bit after high school. As an eight-year-old, Fichtner was crowned Miss Fire Prevention of Greenwich. While a student at Southern Methodist University in Dallas, Texas, Fichtner first became Miss Texas which led to her winning the Miss USA pageant. Fichtner narrowly missed the triple play by finishing as runner-up at the Miss Universe pageant.

"It was textbook. It was almost like you plugged this thing into the traditional American formula. You know, the quarterback and the cheerleader, religious, the whole bit. Doesn't drink, doesn't smoke, does volunteer work, is very into his church yet he's one of the guys. It's something you couldn't write. You really couldn't write it," says Fischetti.

"I guess the only thing that didn't work out is they didn't get married," says Atkins.

To round out his life, Young played guard for the Cardinal varsity basketball team, and he was a pitcher for the baseball team. When he wasn't on the mound, Young was cavorting in center field. He had played the three sports all his life. Now, in high school, he was beginning to get notoriety for his exploits. Young's name began to appear all over the *Greenwich Time* sports section. He was no Dorothy Hamill in the fame department, but his talent as a quarterback, starting guard, and pitcher/center fielder were his starter kit. His straight-A average wasn't hurting him any either.

Along with the publicity came letters from college football coaches, many of them with the return address of an Ivy League school. There was interest because Young was a great athlete and equally talented in the classroom, a prerequisite in that conference regardless of a player's 40-yard-dash time.

Through it all, Young seemed unaffected by the media and recruiting attention. Steve and his younger brother, Mike, still rose every morning at 5 A.M., for the almost-30-mile round trip to Scarsdale, New York, for early morning seminary, their daily Mormon religion class held at the Westchester Ward building. There was always somebody there to make sure the two boys didn't sleep in and miss class. Grit, or Brother Young, as he was called by those attending the class, was the instructor. Each morning Grit, Steve, and Mike would drive to Scarsdale, and an hour later, the three would return home to Split Timber Place. Steve and Mike would then head to school and Grit to the train station for the commute to New York.

"He did that gig where he went to the church in the morning then came to school. Try to do that when you're 16, to get up at 5 o'clock in the morning," adds Fischetti.

Steve was gaining so much acclaim that Mike, jokingly, told people he was the guy with the funny middle name, as in "Mike, Steve Young's Little Brother, Young."

The two boys would have their first chance to "officially" play together in Steve's senior year when both played significant roles on the Greenwich High basketball team. But Mike would always have to follow his brother's legacy on the football field and feel like he had to equal Steve's performances, if not better them. Remarkably, in many instances, Mike did.

Steve was always blazing the trail for his brothers to follow. Already well-known as a great schoolboy athlete, the 1978–79 school year was a coming out for Steve as a player. He was a starter and co-captain in all three sports, with many highlights during each season. In a basketball game against Stamford Catholic won by the Cardinals, Young's jump shot was falling as he knocked down 17 points. During baseball season, he won three games as a starting pitcher, pitching in bad luck a lot of the time. In a game against New Caanan High, Young threw a four-hitter but still took the loss.

As much as Young seemed to thrive playing the two roundball sports, anybody who knew anything realized that basketball and baseball, while enjoyable sidelights for Young, were only time fillers until the football season began. Young knew if he was going to play a sport in college, it was going to be football. As a rule, Grit spoke sparingly to his sons about his own athletic achievements. Still, Steve knew what his father had done as a player, and he often heard his parents speak glowingly of their BYU experiences. Steve grew up following BYU's athletic fortunes, and it was a place he wanted to go to college. When he was younger, he wanted to go to BYU because that's where Mormon kids went. As he got older, his reasons changed. Playing football for the Cougars became a dream.

Because of Young's religion, most of his high school teammates figured the college decision was a foregone conclusion. Young's buddies would see the coaches from various schools at Greenwich's games. BYU's were not among them. But his friends still thought coaches putting the rush on Young were wasting their time. As is usually the case with BYU and its athletic programs, when well-meaning members of the Mormon Church see a player they think is really good, they call someone they know who in turn calls someone on the BYU coaching staff and tells them about their find. More times than not, nothing results from the process. That's essentially how Steve Young and BYU came together. Sort of.

Since Greenwich, Connecticut, wasn't on BYU's regular recruiting route, the Cougar coaches didn't know Steve Young from Brigham Young. It wasn't surprising either. Young was not a throwing quarterback, and although BYU didn't attract many *Street & Smith* all-Americans to Provo, the quarterbacks who did go there were good throwers with a passing background. In the Greenwich offense, it was hard to tell if Young had the makings of a good college quarterback, let alone a we're-throwing-on-every-down BYU quarterback.

The recruiting process with BYU really began when Ted Simmons, president of the Yorktown Stake, the local unit of the Mormon Church made up of a half-dozen wards, the Youngs' included, contacted BYU head coach LaVell Edwards to lobby in Young's behalf. The Simmons family were old friends of the Youngs, with kids close to the same ages as LeGrande and Sherry's kids. Ted Simmons was trying to do Steve a favor, and BYU decided to check out the stake president's story and see if his scouting was any good. Fortunately for Young, the timing of BYU's entrance into the recruiting of the Greenwich High quarterback was impeccable. The scrutiny began as his senior season was unfolding.

• • •

In June before Young's senior year, he and offensive lineman Mike Gasparino were elected team captains for the 1979 season. As captains, they were among the first players to be told by Ornato that he was changing the offense again. The Cardinals were going to the veer. The change in offense wouldn't be as dramatic as the previous year, with the emphasis still on the run and the option. But things would be a little different. So Young had an idea. He realized that spending extra time with Frank Parelli working on the passing game the preceding year had been a huge help. Since Parelli had graduated, and since it looked like Greg Campbell was going to be the go-to receiver (if there was such a thing) in the Cardinals' offense, Young approached Campbell about the two of them working out together in preparation for the season.

"We had the same goal. We just wanted to be the best players and have the best team possible," Campbell says.

For a time that summer, Young had a painting job at the Fichtners before his daily meeting with Campbell. When he put the brush down for the day, Young would show up for some football drills. "We'd throw the ball around and he'd have paint covering him. Steve would throw me the ball, and there would be paint all over it."

The extra work—paint and all—seemed to benefit both players and the team. Greenwich wasn't favored to win any titles, with defending West Division champ Brien McMahon returning 31 players from its title team the previous year. The Cardinals were picked to finish fourth, behind Brien McMahon, Danbury, and Stamford. But

Greenwich started quickly, winning its first four games before dropping a 24-13 decision to Wilton. On a sloppy, wet field against the Warriors, and with Greenwich struggling, Ornato decided to switch Young from quarterback to tailback and change the offense to the power-I in hopes of changing his team's fortunes. Young had clearly come full circle. He had not played any running back since that first year at North Mianus, and here he was lined up behind a quarterback named Grimsich, this time Dave's younger brother Tim. Young was in at tailback for five plays, carrying four times for four yards. Despite the stint at running back, he threw for more yards in that game—179—than any other in his high school career. Campbell caught six of those passes for 105 yards.

"When we would go on the line, we would frequently improvise. When the defensive back would squat down on me, I would take off and basically do a 'go' route. Steve would have to do a lot of scrambling because we didn't have much of a line. But somehow, some way, he would get away from the rush and heave the ball up," says Campbell. "Nine out of ten times I would have to come back for the ball. I would have the defensive back beat deep, and if Steve just hit me in stride I would be in the end zone. But I usually had to come back and jump over the DB's head to make a catch. The funny thing was, this is what the scouts liked when they saw tapes of me coming back and going over guys for the ball. Steve actually did me a great favor by throwing them short."

While Campbell was being recruited by several different schools, Young was also getting the recruiting rush. In his mind, BYU was the place he wanted to go. The only hitch was he was not sure the Cougars were going to have a scholarship for him. Other schools such as Cornell, Virginia, Syracuse, and North Carolina had gift-wrapped offers to Young, yet he was still wavering hoping the Cougars would come through.

Young tried to put the recruiting process out of his mind and concentrate on football. If he continued what he had been doing to that point, everything else would take care of itself. Then disaster struck. On the third play of the homecoming game against Westhill High at Cardinal Stadium, Young took off around right end for 20 yards but came up with a shoulder injury on the tackle. He didn't play another down the rest of the game as Greenwich lost to Westhill, 40-20. It was really the first time Young had ever been injured. Even though the injury wasn't serious, it wasn't much fun watching his team lose while he was standing on the sideline with his helmet in his hand.

Young responded with a 7 for 7 passing performance in a win against Danbury. A 27-0 thrashing of Rippowam followed that. It gave Greenwich the West Division title of the FCIAC, the first time the Cardinals had won their division since 1974. The win earned Greenwich the right to play in the traditional Thanksgiving Day game for the county championship.

Many of the Greenwich players celebrated their victory by congregating at Friendly's, a restaurant in Cos Cob near the school, for a post-game party. It was the popular place to meet and eat and talk about the game. While the players reveled in victory, Ornato thought back to the year Young and his cohorts played JV ball. He remembered how bad they were and how good they had become. In the locker room following the game, Ornato told his team how pessimistic he was about the group at that time, and how wrong he had been.

"I don't know if I've ever had a more determined group or a group with better character. This is one of my most rewarding years of coaching," he told them.

The storybook ending for the team never happened. Greenwich, which had led the league by scoring 215 points in its 7-2 season, never got going in the annual game at Stamford's Boyle Stadium. Young gave an amazing performance anyway. In the final game of his high school career, he rushed for 117 yards and passed for 58 more. That meant Young accounted for 175 of the team's 197 yards of total offense. Mistakes, however, kept Greenwich out of the end zone in the 17-0 loss.

Anybody who saw Young's play that morning knew he was the best quarterback in the FCIAC, and probably the best in the state. Most media outlets agreed, as Young was named by the coaches to the FCIAC's All-West Division squad. The *Bridgeport Post* and *New York Daily News* selected Young to their all-Fairfield County first teams. The crowning achievement came when the National High School Athletic Coaches Association named Young an honorable mention high school all-American.

Unfortunately, there wasn't any time to bask in the glory of it all. Basketball practice had already begun, and Young and Atkins had been elected captains. Young especially had a lot of catching up to do. Atkins was clearly the best player on the team, and he proved it by scoring 28 points and pulling down 14 rebounds in the Cardinals' first game.

"I pretty much knew I was going to get a scholarship to play basketball. It was just a matter of where I was going to play. But I wasn't going to get that scholarship on talent alone. We were going to have to win some ball games, and Steve knew that," says Atkins, who played collegiately at American International College. "In retrospect, I had more fun playing high school basketball than I did college basketball. We were more of a close-knit unit."

Young played well. He averaged in double figures his senior year, topped by a career-high 24-point performance against Ridgefield.

"I thought Steve was a pretty good basketball player. I mean, he started as a junior. He had to be pretty good," says Frank Parelli. "He was a hustler and he always worked very hard at what he was doing."

No matter what sport he was playing, Young would have one performance that transcended all the others. In football, it was his play in the Thanksgiving day game. In basketball it was his 24-point outburst. And in baseball, where—what's new?—Young was one of the team captains, it was not one, but two memorable outings. The first came on May 14 against New Caanan when he no-hit the Rams and walked only one batter in the 3-0 win. Things were going so well for him that he even picked off a runner from third base. He was leading a charmed life. Young added another trophy to his case as his 5-1 record and his .400 batting average were good enough to get him a spot on the All-FCIAC first team.

It got a little ridiculous after that. It seemed no matter what Young did, it was gold. He was a National Honor Society member. He'd been awarded the Harvard Club Book Award, and been recognized with an award by the Society of Women Engineers.

The only thing more absurd than a bunch of female engineers honoring a male student would be a second no-hitter. Before graduation, Young pitched and played the outfield for the Knights of Columbus team in the Greenwich Senior Babe Ruth League. On June 7, he attended Greenwich High's senior prom, then woke up the next day and pitched another no-no. He struck out the side in the first inning, and retired the game's first 10 batters against defending league champion Center Hardware. He added an exclamation point by mowing down the final nine batters he faced. It was an unreal run for Steve Young. He shrugged off his success as ordinary. He never bragged and didn't enjoy the attention his athletic ability brought him. He truly was just one of the guys.

He didn't even have one of those ceremonies in the gym that schools sometimes hold when an athlete signs a letter of intent, with TV cameras and the whole school watching. Instead, Young signed his name at home and dropped the letter in the mail. The letter was on its way to Provo, Utah.

CHAPTER FOUR

Eighth String

For a guy who valued his family more than anything else, going 3,000 miles away to school was the most difficult thing he'd ever done. Provo was only across the country but it might as well have been on the other side of the world.

When Young arrived in Provo, he reported to the football office adjacent to the George Albert Smith Fieldhouse, and scanned the quarterback depth chart for his name. Young wasn't encouraged by what he saw. He finally found STEVE YOUNG in the eighth spot on a quarterback chart that contained only eight names. It didn't take him long to realize the names weren't listed alphabetically. To compound matters, his name was in parentheses. He wondered what the parentheses were for. Was he really eighth string? Was this some kind of cruel joke? Young would say later that his status on the team was "like being in the school choir, but set off in another room to sing alone."

Young's position on the depth chart meant he wouldn't be seeing much action in practice. When he did, he would be facing the first-team defense as the scout team QB, the guy who would run the opposing

teams' offenses. Worse than that, he wouldn't even be allowed to suit up for home games. Instead of standing on
the sideline listening to the adoring crowd cheering on
the Cougars, he would be part of the crowd. The only
football he'd be playing would be on the junior varsity
team.

The move from high school to college was a bigger
adjustment than he had anticipated. In three months'
time, Young had gone from BMOC at Greenwich to
"Who's he?" at BYU.

His low standing among the quarterbacks came as
quite a blow. He had heard about Jim McMahon before
he'd arrived in Provo, and figured two or three other
quarterbacks would be ahead of him. But six? Young
was stunned. Who were all these other quarterbacks,
and how good were they?

Royce Bybee, a senior, was McMahon's backup, the
guy who got most of the garbage time in BYU's routs.
But the guy really being groomed to replace McMahon
was Eric Krzmarzick, a tall, rangy sophomore with a gun
for an arm. BYU offensive coordinator Doug Scovil had
personally recruited Krzmarzick, and he envisioned the
Fallbrook, California, native as the next Marc Wilson. At
6-feet-5, Krzmarzick resembled Wilson and Gifford
Nielsen, another tall, lean BYU quarterback who Scovil
had coached. If there was one thing Scovil liked in a
quarterback, it was height. Scovil wasn't a big McMahon
fan at first because he felt McMahon wasn't tall enough,
but was smitten with Krzmarzick from the very beginning. So confident was Scovil in Krzmarzick's ability that
he'd already formulated this plan: McMahon would play
the 1980 and '81 seasons, and be a high NFL draft pick.
That would leave Krzmarzick to take over in '82 and give

him two years to maintain BYU's high standard of offensive excellence. Krzmarzick, who was being redshirted in 1980, had done his part by tearing it up for the BYU JV team a year earlier. The BYU quarterback line of progression, at least according to Scovil, was already set.

Also in the BYU quarterback mix were Gym Kimball, Mark Haugo, and Mike Jones, who, like Young, would be trying to break through and catch the eyes of LaVell Edwards and Scovil. Although Young was listed as a quarterback, the BYU brain trust looked at him as an athlete first. He wasn't really needed as a quarterback, but he could possibly play another position. Hence the parentheses. The final quarterback of the eight was Ryan Tibbitts, a senior who was more of a wide receiver than a quarterback. Still, he'd played some QB in junior college and on the BYU JV team, so he was listed with the quarterbacks.

That first year, Young did get to play quarterback on the JV team, splitting time with Kimball and Haugo. At practice, Scovil rarely acknowledged Young. The pecking order at BYU had been established and all Young could do was try to improve his position.

"Scovil has no use for freshmen," says Danny Plater, a BYU wide receiver from 1978–81 who was recruited by Scovil. "You've got to pay your dues. Scovil didn't like that Young came from an option offense in high school, had never really thrown the ball, and didn't know much about the pass offense. Scovil thought it would be too much of an undertaking to teach Young to be a BYU quarterback. Plus he hadn't recruited Young."

"That was an era when Scovil liked the tall quarterback," says Kimball, himself only 6-feet-1. "That was a problem for Young because he wasn't really tall. He was also a much better runner than thrower. Because he ran so well it almost made him look like a worse thrower than he actually was." Young had a big hill to climb. He was a quarterback with a wishbone pedigree trying to break in at a school with one of the most sophisticated passing offenses in the nation. No wonder Young was barely a blip on the BYU football screen.

The most highly recruited player from that class of 1980 was Waymon Hamilton, a running back from Calipatria, California, with the kind of speed BYU rarely attracted at that position. Also in the 1980 recruiting class was a tight end from Kennewick, Washington, who had moved to the Salt Lake City suburb of Sandy after the football season of his senior year. Gordon Hudson was 6-feet-4, a bit on the skinny side, with decent speed. It didn't take Young long to learn Hudson had a great pair of hands.

Hudson had gotten recruiting nibbles from a variety of schools, including BYU, but he didn't attract much attention beyond some letters and occasional phone calls. The only Division I schools to actively recruit Hudson were Washington State and Utah State, and even Washington State's interest was tepid at best. In the end, neither school offered Hudson a scholarship. As national letter of intent day approached, Hudson decided Division I-AA football was probably the best he could do, and made a tentative decision to go to the University of Montana, where the Grizzlies wanted him as a defensive back.

At the last minute, Hudson sent game film of himself to the BYU coaching staff, mainly because he was a Mormon and because BYU was located only 25 miles from his new home.

Watching the film, LaVell Edwards' interest was piqued enough for him to dispatch an assistant coach to Brighton High School in Sandy to watch Hudson play basketball. BYU came away from the basketball game suitably impressed with Hudson's athleticism, his good hands, and his footwork. On the first day national letters of intent could be signed, the Cougars offered the tight end/power forward a scholarship, which Hudson gratefully accepted. In Young and Hudson, Edwards had unknowingly bagged what would become one of the most prolific passing and receiving combinations in the history of college football. So much for the theory about blue-chip recruits.

It didn't take long for Young to meet Hudson. Most of the freshmen football players lived in Helaman Halls, an eight-hall dormitory immediately south of Cougar Stadium on campus. Young moved into Taylor Hall where he was assigned to live with Keith Arbon, a wide receiver from Boise, Idaho, who, like Young, wondered what his football future held. The two freshmen would stay up late in their dorm, talking about football, the LDS Church, girls, and missions. Arbon wasn't convinced a mission was for him, while Young was. The disappointing way things had begun in his college football career left Young feeling like a mission might come sooner than later. If he was going to be homesick, Young figured he might as well be homesick knocking on doors preaching the gospel instead of having to suffer through the indignity of not even being able to dress for home games.

That first semester, Young rarely left his dorm except for classes, practice, and church. He didn't socialize much at all, but then he hardly had time. He was taking 14-and-a-half hours that first semester, a heavy load for a freshman, heavier still for a freshman athlete. With school demanding a lot of Young's time, it seemed like he would have no time to worry about football. But he did worry and spent a lot of time on the phone talking to his parents in Greenwich. He'd also talk a lot with Mike, his younger brother. Football wasn't going well for him, either. In a Saturday morning scrimmage in New Rochelle, New York, Mike, who was hoping to fill his brother's big shoes as the Cardinals' quarterback, broke his right forearm a week before the season-opener against Warde High School, and was lost for the season.

So Young immersed himself in his homework, and never went to John Hall, the place to see and be seen if you were a football player. It was in John Hall that Haugo and three other freshmen football players, Ty Mattingly, Brad Smith, and Adam Haysbert, set up camp in a huge room called the Overflow that usually accommodated extra students who didn't have specific dorm assignments. Since the Overflow wasn't being used in the fall semester of 1980, the four players claimed it and watched as it became the unofficial hangout for the athletes who lived in Helaman. Young rarely visited. He was too lonely and frustrated to do much socializing.

BYU had gone undefeated during the 1979 regular season, moving into the top 10 for the first time in school history. As an encore, the Cougars' 1980 season would surpass 1979 in both excitement and success. Scovil, who had left BYU for an assistant coaching position with the NFL's Cincinnati Bengals after 1979, changed his mind and returned as the Cougars' offensive coordinator in February. McMahon loved Scovil's wide-open attack, and Scovil grew to appreciate McMahon and his abilities, even if he wasn't 6-feet-5.

Scovil was getting pretty spoiled. In his career, he had tutored Roger Staubach at Navy, and Gifford Nielsen, Marc Wilson, and now McMahon at BYU. Of the four, McMahon may very well have been the best of the bunch. In the 1980 season, McMahon was unstoppable as he obliterated many NCAA records while passing for 4,571 yards. BYU attracted 41,000-plus fans per game in 30,000-seat Cougar Stadium, and was rolling. With all these good things happening, the last thing any true-blue BYU fan cared about was a lonely and homesick freshman wishbone quarterback.

All Young could do was bide his time, work hard in practice, and slowly try to make his way up the depth chart. Realistically, with so many good quarterbacks ahead of him, Young wondered whether he'd ever get a shot to play. To compound matters, Young had been approached by Edwards and assistant coach Dick Felt about becoming a defensive back. Edwards couldn't overlook Young's blazing speed and athleticism. Edwards realized that Young wasn't a very accomplished thrower, so considered it a waste to keep a burner like him at quarterback when he could really make an impact in the secondary. Plus, Scovil kept telling Edwards that Krzmarzick and Haugo were the quarterbacks of the future. So Young listened politely to the defensive back discussions, and he even began working with teammate Tom Holmoe, one of BYU's starting cornerbacks, on his footwork and backpedaling technique. Young went along with it all, but he was certain he hadn't traveled across the country to play defensive back and give up the position he'd played his entire life. A month after arriving in Provo, Young was to happiness what BYU was to caffeine. He began to weigh his options.

He could quit the team, forget about football, and concentrate on school. He could leave BYU, return to Greenwich, and attend a school closer to home. Going on a mission was also a viable possibility. He could be gone for two years, return and hope the logjam at quarterback might be alleviated. Young's final option was to stay in Provo and stick it out with the hope the football situation would get better. Of course there was no guarantee that things would improve.

On September 19, 1980, the BYU junior varsity team, nicknamed the Kittens, opened its season by hosting Ricks (Junior) College in Cougar Stadium. Gym Kimball started at quarterback and completed 13 of his 29 passes for 198 yards. Kimball was a freshman in eligibility, but a year older than Young because he had skipped the 1979–80 school year after breaking his leg before the '79 season. Head JV coach Lance Reynolds finally pulled Kimball late in the game and replaced him with Young, who did his best work on the ground, rushing for 35 yards on three carries in the 28-21 win. Young's play wasn't anything special. He did what he did best; he ran and he ran well.

The following week the Kittens traveled to Ephraim, Utah, for a game against Snow (Junior) College. The Badgers jumped ahead early and held a 10-point lead entering the fourth period when Young made another relief appearance. Kimball had started and thrown for a touchdown before giving way to Young. Young led a Kittens comeback. He scored on a three-yard quarterback sneak with under eight minutes to play, and then found Gordon Hudson for a two-point conversion to give BYU the 39-38 lead that would become the final score. The Young-to-Hudson music had begun. It had a definite resonance to it, and Young finally had a reason to smile.

By the midway point of the season, Kimball, Young, and Haugo were all getting playing time in the JV games. Young and Kimball both felt Haugo was ahead of them because Haugo was Scovil's fair-haired boy. Young also felt Kimball was a notch above him because Kimball was getting the most playing time of any of the quarterbacks. It was a big guessing game. The only thing they knew for sure was that Mike Jones, a sophomore, was not in BYU's future plans. Jones had already begun the transfer process that would take him to Cal-Lutheran after the 1980 season. Ryan Tibbitts was never a serious quarterback contender. The Big Six were McMahon, Bybee, Krzmarzick, and then in no particular order, Young, Haugo, and Kimball.

Each day at practice, Scovil would work with the first team, but would also find extra instruction time for Krzmarzick and Haugo. One of Scovil's favorite things to do was send a quarterback to his dorm and have him pose in front of a mirror without a ball. This, he would tell the player, would help him get a picture in his mind of what a Scovil-taught quarterback was supposed to look like in his set up, his throw, and his follow-through.

"That was probably Scovil's biggest strength. He could literally take a snapshot of your motion in his mind and then be able to find a weakness. He was such a perfectionist," says Haugo. "On the field, Scovil would monitor every throw, making sure the quarterback's thumb snapped down on release, and that the height of his elbow when he cocked and released the ball was correct. Scovil would even coach his guys how to take the ball from center." Krzmarzick and Haugo got that attention. Kimball and Young did not.

"It was hostile the way Scovil acted toward me and Young," says Kimball. "Scovil would bring up a point in a team meeting and he'd say, 'Did you hear that, Kimball? I want to be sure to repeat it for you.' He'd say that kind of thing all the time."

Scovil's treatment of Young wasn't much different.

Once during practice, Scovil became frustrated with Young's play and, in front of the entire offensive team, asked, "What are you playing quarterback for?" Scovil then told Young to leave and go across the field to join the defense. Embarrassed, Young did what he was told, while a lot of the veterans stood there and laughed. "I thought it was atrocious," recalls Kimball.

It wasn't a great environment for Young and Kimball, and even though Kimball was listed as the third-string QB, he knew it was merely window dressing while Krzmarzick redshirted. It was quite a come-down for both Young and Kimball, who had arrived at BYU with high hopes. Young could have been at any number of schools in the east, and Kimball, who had originally planned to go to the University of Utah, wondered if he shouldn't have cast his lot with the Utes. At least somewhere else, the quarterback coach might like them. "It was horrible. It was the equivalent of having your parents die and being put in a foster home where the people there couldn't stand you," says Kimball.

Young and Kimball kept quiet about their dissatisfaction with the way things were going. They'd talk together, but they rarely took their complaints to other teammates. Instead Kimball kept in steady contact with his parents in Salt Lake City, and Young rolled up a big long-distance bill to Greenwich. When nothing else was going right, Young knew he could turn to his parents. His mom and dad would offer words of encouragement, and Young would temporarily feel better.

Despite the hardships, Young still got his share of good fortune. It started when BYU began preparing for its game with Wyoming. The Cowboys ran the wishbone, so Edwards and Scovil called on Young to be the scout team quarterback and replicate Wyoming's triple option in practice. Running the wishbone was something Young did with ease.

Later that week, while the varsity hosted Wyoming, the Kittens traveled to Las Vegas for a game with Nevada-Las Vegas. Against the Rebels, Young was given his first starting assignment, and BYU, the most pass-happy team in the nation, came out running the wishbone. On their first drive, in searing 95-degree heat in the Silver Bowl, Young ran, pitched, and handed off in an offense that completely mystified the Rebel JV squad. When Kimball and Haugo took their turns, BYU went back to the pro set. Kimball threw a touchdown pass, but it was Haugo who lit up UNLV like so many casino marquees. He threw three touchdown passes in the short time he was at the helm, and played the kind of football everybody dreams of playing as the Kittens routed the Rebels.

"That game for me was almost magical. I remember it felt like I couldn't do anything wrong. I didn't play that much, but it seemed that it went real well," says Haugo. "I think that game set in my mind that I might be the next quarterback in line after Krzmarzick."

Not long after that game came a bombshell. The Holiday Bowl in San Diego would be the last game for

Doug Scovil at BYU. He had accepted the head coaching job at San Diego State.

The Aztecs had been pummelled by BYU year in and year out since joining the Western Athletic Conference, so when Claude Gilbert was given his walking papers as SDSU's coach, Scovil was the guy San Diego State officials wanted. They watched BYU's offensive pyrotechnics each December when BYU made its annual trek to the Holiday Bowl, and they decided Scovil could help change that trend. Ultimately, Scovil leaving BYU facilitated the emergence of Steve Young. It was as if the Aztecs had laid out the red carpet and tossed rose petals at Young's feet.

Young and Kimball were in the locker room when they heard the news about Scovil, and they were both positively giddy. They didn't even try to mask their excitement. As the two quarterbacks walked through the fieldhouse, Kimball yelled to no one in particular, "He's gone. He's gone." Haugo, who was within earshot, heard Kimball and knew who he was talking about. Moments later, both Haugo and Krzmarzick found out their mentor was leaving. It was Christmas for Young and Kimball, April Fools' Day for Krzmarzick and Haugo.

"After that I kind of had a sinking feeling that my days there were numbered," recalls Haugo. "Scovil had flat-out told me and had insinuated that I was next. I think both Steve and Gym felt that I was the favorite son."

Despite not having suited up for any varsity home games, Young and Haugo were notified they would be able to travel with the varsity to San Diego for the Holiday Bowl against Southern Methodist.

In San Diego, Young and Haugo roomed together, while Ryan Tibbitts and Kimball shared a room in the

Mission Bay Hilton. None of the four felt any pressure. The only real work was practice, and even that wasn't exactly taxing as McMahon and Bybee were getting most of the reps. Young ran SMU's offense, trying his best to simulate the play of Lance McIlhenny, the SMU quarterback. Other than the practices and meetings, Young, Kimball, and Haugo were basically along for the ride, and Young did his best to enjoy himself as only Young could. Whenever the Cougars had free time, Young planted himself in front of a complimentary pinball machine in the team's hotel. What more could Young ask for?

When the bowl game finally rolled around, the freshmen QBs, none of whom were listed on the Cougars' roster in the program, stood on the Jack Murphy Stadium sideline and watched Jim McMahon bring the Cougars back from a 45-25 deficit with 4:07 to play, capping the comeback with a scintillating 46-yard touchdown pass with no time left on the clock. Incredibly, BYU beat SMU 46-45. It should have been a satisfying finish to Young's first year. It wasn't.

Young had traveled with the varsity and suited up for a game, he played pinball at his leisure, took home all sorts of gifts, visited Sea World, toured a Navy aircraft carrier, soaked in the warm California sun, and had a new quarterback coach to look forward to. He had also played reasonably well in his JV action, and to top it off, he was witness to one of college football's greatest quarterbacks pulling off one of the great comebacks of all time. But as Young traveled to Greenwich for the remainder of the Christmas break, he wasn't exactly decking the halls. Instead he was contemplating his plight. His BYU experience was turning out to be something less than he hoped it would be.

When Steve was still in high school, on the long, early morning rides to Scarsdale for seminary, he'd sit in the car and think. He'd make a lot of decisions during those rides and then ask his father for his opinion. It had been a while, but it was time to bounce a new idea off of Grit. Steve Young wanted to quit playing football for BYU.

The decision to quit had been an incredibly difficult one, and Young needed someone to talk to. He needed someone to either confirm his decision or talk him out of it.

"Dad, I've had it with this whole thing. I'm not having fun; I'm not enjoying myself. I think I'm going to quit," Steve said.

"Son, you can quit, but you can't come home. I don't live with quitters." The stoic father wasn't budging on this one. Steve could do all the quitting he wanted; he just couldn't do it and then take refuge at 27 Split Timber Place. The old fullback, who used to battle and fight for every yard when he was playing, had spoken.

So Grit Young's kid returned to Provo with the intent to do his best at spring practice and let whatever was going to happen happen.

• • •

Replacing Scovil on BYU's coaching staff was Ted Tollner, a former quarterback at Cal-Poly and an assistant coach on Claude Gilbert's San Diego State staff who had been pink-slipped along with the rest of the Aztec assistants when Scovil rolled into town. LaVell Edwards hired Tollner to tutor the Cougar quarterbacks and keep the offense on cruise control.

Not long after Tollner began his new job, he was walking through the Smith Fieldhouse where quarterbacks and receivers often worked out together. Tollner was really only familiar with McMahon when he took the job, having coached against him the previous year at San Diego State. The other BYU quarterbacks were merely names to him at this point. Tollner stopped to watch the players and noticed a curly-headed guy with a nice release throwing the ball. Tollner inquired about the quarterback, then immediately walked to Edwards' office. Based on a couple of Steve Young's throws, Tollner saw potential and talent that Doug Scovil didn't or wouldn't. With Tollner on board, Young would not be playing in the BYU defensive backfield anytime soon.

The discovery of Young set off a chain of events leading to Young's meteoric rise on the BYU depth chart and hastening the departure of Haugo, Kimball, and, yes, even Krzmarzick.

Before 1981 spring practice began, Haugo, wide receiver Glen Kozlowski, and tight end Stan Pulu drove to Kozlowski's family's home in Carlsbad, California, with the idea they would follow Scovil to San Diego State. "Scovil told me I would always have a place at San Diego State. I didn't care if Scovil had gone to the west coast of Africa to coach. I would have followed him there," Haugo says. His decision to transfer had pretty much been decided.

Young played extremely well in the annual Blue-White intrasquad game, and he was making dramatic improvements in his play. He seemed much more relaxed with Scovil out of the picture. Plus, Young was beginning to feel what it was like to be the guy favored by the quarterback coach.

Kimball also saw time in the Blue-White game, and he did nothing that would move him up or down the depth chart. Kimball could see what was happening. His initial excitement about Scovil's departure was tempered when Tollner took an instant shine to Young. "Tollner came in and liked Steve and liked his style. When Tollner came in, he was as pro-Steve Young as Scovil had been for Krzmarzick. And Tollner was as much adverse to Krzmarzick as Scovil had been toward Young," says Kimball.

That became clear when Young was named the junior varsity most valuable player for 1980 at the spring awards banquet. Kimball was astounded. No one quarterback had been any better than the other two, and considering the team also had Gordon Hudson, linebacker Todd Shell, and Waymon Hamilton to choose from, the selection of Young as MVP didn't seem right to Kimball.

By then, the decision had been made. Steve Young would back up McMahon in 1981. Young probably didn't deserve the MVP, but it was a convenient way to validate the coaching staff's decision to go with Young as the backup.

Before fall practice began in August of 1981, Young's sophomore season, Haugo and Jones were gone, Kimball sensed he would follow Haugo's lead and look for a place to transfer, and Eric Krzmarzick, who as recently as six months earlier seemed like the better-than-even-money favorite to replace McMahon, returned from California and began working out with BYU's receivers, who had also reported back to school early. "We'd throw at night, and Krzmarzick had this hitch in his release. It was terrible. He would wrap the ball almost under his armpit before releasing it," recalls wide receiver Danny Plater. "I was thinking, What's going on? When I first saw him do it I thought he was goofing off. He wasn't, and he couldn't get rid of the hitch. He was done. He couldn't do a thing after that. I mean, it took him so long to get rid of the ball. Even if you're talking a hundredth of a second, that means a lot when you're in the pocket. His hitch took longer than a hundredth of a second."

"It was almost like a spasmodic motion," says Kimball of Krzmarzick's throwing problems. "I don't know where he picked it up or what caused it—if it was psychological or what—but it was an unbelievable change. He had a pure motion, a beautiful motion. Then all of a sudden this ghost just crept up in his motion."

Edwards also noticed what was happening to Krzmarzick, and knew something radical had occurred. The air was being let out of the heir apparent.

The stage was now set. The original list of eight quarterbacks had been pared to four, and of those four, Krzmarzick's game had gone in the tank, Kimball was contemplating a transfer, and McMahon was preparing for the millions some NFL team would soon be offering. More important than that, at least for Young, was that Scovil was nowhere to be found in Provo. There would be no more scout team play for Young. He was the backup quarterback at Brigham Young University, and the Christmas-time discussion with Grit a few months earlier seemed eons old.

CHAPTER FIVE

The Backup

BYU's sports programs seemed blessed during the 1980–81 school year. Jim McMahon had pretty much transcended the position of quarterback, and Danny Ainge, the professional baseball player, was pointing out to the basketball world that he was a pretty fair hoops player too. His length-of-the-court dash that resulted in the game-winning shot against Notre Dame in the NCAA tournament was tantamount to the football team's win in the Holiday Bowl. Things were pretty peachy in Provo, and McMahon and Ainge were the main reasons.

By 1981, Ainge's eligibility had expired, leaving McMahon alone in the Cougar athletic fishbowl. Because of his football exploits, McMahon could do no wrong on the BYU campus. Yes, McMahon was a Catholic attending a Mormon school; yes, he chewed tobacco, drank beer, and cussed on a regular basis, all no-nos at BYU. McMahon also had a habit of winning football games, and he had a flair for the dramatic, as evidenced by his "Save the Game" pass against SMU, which did just that. So what if, in the minds of BYU fans, he had a few, uh, faults? The 1980 season had brought the Cougars their first bowl win in history, and they were looking for more in 1981. Fans could marvel at McMahon for one more season, and they planned to. They weren't even worrying about the future.

Very few knew about the machinations as the heirs apparent battled for the backup quarterback spot. All they knew was that Young had emerged from the derby with the prize. But it hardly mattered, at least not in 1981. To the fans, Steve Young was just another Royce Bybee or Mark Giles or Jeff Duva, backup Cougar quarterbacks of years past who only saw action when BYU had built 30-point leads anyway. McMahon was the man and that was what was important. Steve Young was still a nobody at Brigham Young University, even if the place was named for his great-great-great grandfather.

For LaVell Edwards, the backup quarterback business was a little more serious. Like any coach, Edwards was always looking ahead. The Cougar coach was happy to have McMahon back for one more season; however, he knew somebody was going to have to captain the ship in 1982. Edwards hoped Ted Tollner was right about Young.

Meanwhile, BYU was a metronome, never skipping a beat. The Cougars opened the 1981 season nursing a 12-game winning streak, which they quickly extended to 15 by beating up on Long Beach State, Air Force, and Texas-El Paso. Young played in the UTEP and Long Beach State games, getting mop-up duty after a standing ovation sent McMahon to the sidelines. In the 65-8 pasting of UTEP, in which Young threw his first touchdown as a college football player (a seven-yarder to wideout Kirk Pendleton), Krzmarzick also saw his first varsity action, completing 1 of 3 passes. Everybody played,

and everybody had fun. After all, the opponent was
UTEP, and BYU recognized that it had a lot more latitude
against the Miners than it did against most teams. So
much latitude that Ryan Tibbitts, the sometimes quarterback, played defensive back for a couple of plays late in
the fourth quarter.

After the win over UTEP, the Cougars moved to
11th in the Associated Press Top 20. BYU was on the fast
track with a legitimate Heisman Trophy candidate; they
were quickly becoming a major college football power.
Young was trying to learn as much as he could before
McMahon inevitably took his act to the National Football
League.

• • •

As the chartered plane touched down at Stapleton
International Airport in Denver, the BYU football team
boarded two buses that took it straight to Folsom Field
on the campus of the University of Colorado in Boulder.
It was a typical road game routine for the Cougars.
Instead of going to the hotel, the team went straight to
Folsom for a walk-through, no-pads practice Friday after-
noon, September 25.

Colorado and BYU had met nine previous times on
the football field, mostly in the 1930s and '40s, with BYU
not worrying as much about winning as it did scoring in
those games. The Cougars were shut out in four of those
nine contests. By 1981, the tide had shifted as Colorado's
program fell on hard times, and BYU experienced never-
before-seen success. Hoping for a rejuvenation similar to
BYU's, Colorado hired Chuck Fairbanks away from the
NFL's New England Patriots to coach the Buffs.
Fairbanks' arrival hadn't helped. Colorado was 1-10 in

1980, and BYU was a prohibitive favorite going into the September 26 game between the two old rivals.

Still, BYU was from the WAC and Colorado, the Big Eight. BYU rarely played non-conference games against opponents from prestigious conferences, and that made this game very important to BYU's players and coaches. A win against a Big Eight school would do a lot for the program.

On game day, bright sunshine greeted BYU. As the players trotted out onto the artificial turf right before kickoff, Steve Young heard a familiar voice.

"Hey, Steve, welcome to the Big Eight." Doing the yelling was Young's pass-catching mate from Greenwich, Greg Campbell. The second-string wide receiver, whose move up the Colorado depth chart had been as precipitous as Young's on BYU's, had a big smile on his face. Young pointed toward Campbell, grinned, and headed toward the sideline where he figured to remain for the rest of the game. It seemed doubtful that Young would see any action. He was wrong on both counts.

It was vintage McMahon in the early going as he hit Danny Plater for a 44-yard touchdown pass on the game's opening series, giving the Cougars a 7-0 lead. In the second quarter, BYU's all-American center Bart Oates broke his ankle and had to take a seat on the bench. But even without Oates, BYU led 17-0 at halftime, and showed no signs of letting up. Early in the third quarter, McMahon hit Glen Kozlowski (who decided not to transfer to San Diego State) for another TD to move BYU ahead 24-0. It was not long after that score that Young quickly had a sick feeling in his stomach, along with many Cougar fans.

On a quick slant pass, McMahon tried to jump while he threw and was hit on the right side of his knee as he released the ball. He crumpled to the ground in pain.

Plater, McMahon's best friend, was scared, and the rest of the Cougar players also realized the seriousness of the injury. The concern Plater saw on his friend's face told him that McMahon's knee was in a bad way. As the medical personnel attended to the BYU meal ticket, Young quickly warmed up on the sideline. He had no time to think about what was happening. Ted Tollner told him he was the man. On the opposing sideline, Campbell knew Young was going in, so he immediately walked over to defensive coordinator Doug Knotts. Knowing the Colorado defense had not prepared for Young, and really knew very little about the left-handed backup quarterback, Campbell gave Knotts a quick scouting report.

"You better put someone on him at all times. This guy is going to be running the ball a lot," Campbell said.

Knotts didn't seem too concerned. In a way, he was relieved. BYU, he figured, couldn't be as effective with McMahon on the bench.

On the first series after the injury, Young took BYU 65 yards in four plays in a style BYU fans would come to appreciate during the next two seasons. It was a quintessential Steve Young drive. On the first play, Young hit Kozlowski for 27 yards. On the second, he scrambled out of the pocket and ran for another 29. Then Young hit tight end Gordon Hudson for an 11-yard TD pass. Forty-nine seconds had elapsed. Campbell stood on the sidelines feeling like he was back at Greenwich High. He decided it was a lot more fun playing with Young than against him.

It was an ideal situation for Young to enter a game. BYU had a big lead, Young wouldn't have to throw the ball a lot, and all he had to do was keep the offense moving. That he did as BYU cruised to the 44-20 victory.

In the locker room, much of the attention was on Young, the unknown who had come in and played admirably replacing McMahon. During the post-game interviewing process, word got out who Young's great-great-great grandfather was. It was the elusive angle any sportswriter looks for. Once it became public knowledge that Steve Young was kin to Brigham Young, he became a walking, talking parenthetical sentence, as in "Steve Young, great-great-great grandson of Mormon church president Brigham Young, . . ."

The attention was very new for Young. He gave the reporters his "Ah shucks" routine, and was extremely humble as he talked about getting his chance under some tough circumstances. He also admitted how nervous he was when he first entered the game. If his confession was true, it didn't show. Young had played well, even if his stats weren't overly impressive. He finished the game completing 4 of 10 passes for 63 yards with two touchdowns, the scoring toss to Hudson, and a 22-yard strike to Plater. Young proved Campbell's sideline scouting report to be an accurate one. His final rushing tally: 61 yards on four carries, and an adeptness at avoiding the rush in the pocket. In the Cougars' locker room, Young couldn't have been happier about his play. The completion percentage wasn't what he would have liked. But the touchdown passes felt very good, and his running of the ball was just like old times. He'd passed the test, no pun intended.

"What Young pulled off in that first game at Colorado was tremendous. At BYU, it was pretty much expected that the quarterback was going to come in, get the job done, and make it happen. Personally, there was no thought or trepidation in terms of whether Young could get the job done. We just assumed he could," says Plater. "He came in and did a great job. I could see he was nervous, but that nervousness is what gives you the edge. It translates into concentration and focus."

Says Calvin Close, the Cougars' starting left guard on that '81 team, "I guess there might have been a little bit of a letdown after Jim got hurt simply because Jim McMahon was the kind of leader who had the whole offense believing there would be no way of stopping us from scoring. I think when Steve came in there was naturally a little bit of a letdown because we hadn't played with him as much as we had with McMahon. But Steve has a lot of athletic ability. He was able to run the ball so well."

In the minutes following the game, Tollner took Young aside and told him there was a good chance he would get his first start at quarterback against Utah State. On the bus ride back to Denver and on the plane trip to Salt Lake City, Young wasn't exactly the picture of relaxation. The severity of McMahon's injury was still in question, and nobody would know for another 24 hours whether McMahon would be ready for the Cougars' next game. Based on what he had already heard, Young figured he would be BYU's new starting quarterback, at least temporarily.

When Young returned home that night, he heard some more good news. Mike, making his first start as Greenwich High's quarterback, passed for 109 yards and rushed for an identical amount, on the strength of 55-, 52-, and one-yard touchdown runs in the Cardinals' 33-14 win against Rippowam High. It had been a very productive weekend for the Young boys.

Steve quickly learned what it was like to have the spotlight shining on him. By Sunday afternoon, Young learned McMahon was definitely out of the Utah State game. The timing of all this wasn't ideal, and Young knew it. Because of LDS Church general conference, a twice-a-year gathering of church leaders and members to be held Saturday and Sunday in Salt Lake City, BYU officials had already scheduled the home game with Utah State for Friday night so it wouldn't conflict with conference. With Sunday an off day for BYU, Young had just four days to prepare for his starting debut.

Utah State coach Bruce Snyder wasn't convinced Young was the guy BYU would put out on the field to run the offense. Snyder fully expected McMahon to play, and he prepared his team accordingly. Snyder could prepare all he wanted, but McMahon was not going to play. He wasn't even going to suit up. No tears were found inside McMahon's injured knee, but it remained swollen. And although McMahon practiced toward the end of the week, he couldn't meet the sprinting requirements that would have cleared him to play.

Nothing much changed that week for BYU. Young was the new quarterback but it was business as usual. The Cougars would pass and pass often. The only changes were some roll outs that Tollner added to take advantage of Young's running ability.

While everything was pretty much status quo with the team, it wasn't a normal week for Young. He didn't sleep well, and his nerves were killing him. When McMahon's injury thrust Young into a playing situation against Colorado, he didn't have time to think about it and psyche himself out. He had plenty of time to do that leading up to the Utah State game. Young's clean, solid performance in almost an entire half against Colorado didn't help matters. BYU quarterback Gifford Nielsen had gone down with a knee injury in the middle of the 1976 season, and Cougar fans watched Marc Wilson replace him effortlessly. Wilson then went on to carve out his own niche in BYU football history. The BYU fans, pretty spoiled by this point, fully expected Young to come in and roll up 500 yards of total offense, lead the team to 40-plus points, and win by four touchdowns. Fans expected not a good, but a great performance from Young.

"I think everybody—the fans, myself, the football team, and perhaps maybe a few of the coaches—was unfair. How could you expect Young to go in and do what McMahon had done? I mean, he wasn't even 20 years old yet," says Plater. "He was a sophomore kid who had never played, and the expectations were so high it was almost impossible for him to succeed."

But he did, and not in the ordinary BYU-by-30 way people had become accustomed to. Young left a few things for the very end.

In the rare night game at Cougar Stadium, BYU struggled with Utah State. When the Aggies' Maurice Turner scored on a six-yard sweep with 5:53 remaining in the game to give the Aggies a 26-20 lead, the lights on BYU's 17-game winning streak began to dim. Young, however, would not let it happen.

BYU took over the ball on its own 37 and began marching. Young wasn't calm, and he wasn't hyper. He was focused. The key plays were completions of 17 and 16 yards to Plater and Gordon Hudson that helped set up a Waymon Hamilton touchdown run. A missed extra point kept the game tied until Cougar linebacker Todd Shell intercepted a pass and returned it 12 yards for the game-winning touchdown. Young's initial start was a success, and it showed in the Associated Press poll as BYU climbed to the number eight slot. A BYU team had never been ranked that high.

Nevada-Las Vegas was next up on the Cougars' schedule, and BYU expected another win. Although McMahon was healthy enough to play against the Rebels, he was kept out since UNLV was a non-league opponent. Young's solid play had also figured into the decision to hold out McMahon. The only negative with Young, besides his inexperience, was his immaturity in reading defenses. Young often had trouble detecting what a defense was doing when it put in a wrinkle or two he hadn't seen before. That problem reared its head against UNLV.

On a windy afternoon in Cougar Stadium, Young played like a guy who had one-and-a-half games of big-time college football to his credit. Young was 21 for 40, passing for a respectable 269 yards, and the team posted 41 points. He also threw four interceptions, and the Cougar defense allowed UNLV to amass 628 yards of total offense and 45 points. Without much warning, the winning streak was history and the questions about Young's abilities began.

Says Plater, "Steve didn't throw the ball that well, but it wasn't just Steve's fault. It was a lot of people's. He certainly put up the numbers to win. We just let a team that was nowhere near our caliber score too many points."

It was a stunning upset for everybody involved, and among a spate of disappointed players Young was easily the most frustrated and upset by the loss. He felt as if he'd let the team down.

"Here's the thing. How is it that everybody gets down on Steve Young after that game when you look at the numbers he put up? People were just used to this high-efficiency offense with very few breakdowns," says Plater.

The loss hastened the reemergence of McMahon into the BYU lineup for its game against San Diego State. Young would watch from the sidelines, missing his chance to show Scovil what he could do. McMahon would have the honors of putting the wood to Young's former antagonist. As for Young, he would throw only four more passes the rest of the year, all in mop-up situations.

In the two-and-a-half games Young played, his stats weren't bad. He completed 56 of his 111 passes for 731 yards, threw five interceptions and passed for five touchdowns. Young had faced his crucible and acquitted himself well. He proved he could step in with the pressure on. He couldn't wait for the 1982 season to begin.

CHAPTER SIX

The Starter

For a church that emphasizes genealogy as much as The Church of Jesus Christ of Latter-day Saints, it was only fitting that one of its most interesting family trees was one that included five men not related by blood at all. Their relation came from holding the title BYU QUARTERBACK.

In 1974, LaVell Edwards decided the only way BYU could ever win on a consistent basis was to throw the ball. Edwards had watched Virgil Carter shred defenses when he was quarterbacking the Cougars in the 1960s, convincing BYU's defensive coordinator that the forward pass was the way to go. He just needed to get the players and the coaches who could implement the offense. The LaVell Edwards era began with two non-descript years of mainly running the ball. Then BYU convinced quarterback Gary Sheide, a junior college transfer, to enroll at the Provo school. Sheide threw the ball all over the field, and garnered some national attention, but BYU football was an unknown entity at the time and Sheide toiled in anonymity outside the intermountain west. But BYU was on its pass-happy way. Sheide led the Cougars to their first bowl appearance, satisfying Edwards that his decision to change the offense had been a correct one. He was on to something very, very good.

When Sheide graduated, a BYU basketball player from Provo, Gifford Nielsen, changed sports and became an instant success throwing instead of shooting his ball of choice. Nielsen was such an accomplished successor to Sheide that he ended up playing six years with the Houston Oilers.

Before he departed, Nielsen spawned Marc Wilson, who took BYU to its first undefeated regular season and more national recognition. Wilson's claim to fame was that he was BYU's first first-round NFL draft choice.

One QB breaking records from a heretofore small-time football school would be considered a fluke. Two QBs doing it, okay. But three? Somebody was obviously doing something right. That somebody was Edwards, who had a knack for hiring innovative offensive minds and giving them free reign. It didn't hurt that Edwards had also attracted talented guys to stand over center, do the seven-step drop, and pick apart opposing defenses.

By Wilson's senior year, the line of quarterbacks that traced back to Sheide began to take on a life of its own, and each subsequent BYU quarterback would feel the pressure of living up to the previous quarterbacks' accomplishments.

After Wilson came Jim McMahon, who outperformed all of them before becoming BYU's second first-round draft choice, and eventually BYU's first Super Bowl quarterback. McMahon then passed the mantle of responsibility to Steve Young, who learned quickly what it was like to stand in the spotlight and try to carry on the proud quarterback tradition at Brigham Young University.

In Young family history, Brigham Young may have been Steve Young's great-great-great-grandfather. But in the genealogy of BYU football Gary Sheide carried the same title.

• • •

When BYU named Young its starter, it was safe to say that none of the previous quarterbacks had a larger shadow to live in than the one from which Young would have to emerge. All the other quarterbacks had been great players, but McMahon was an entirely different animal. McMahon had an innate ability to see the entire field, and read defenses. He would call audibles 60 percent of the time, and make it look so easy that people would forget how complicated the BYU offense actually was. The shadow McMahon cast was at least as big as nearby Mount Timpanogos. In his two years as a full-time starter, McMahon lost two games, and he was the only BYU quarterback to ever lead his team to a bowl win, something he did twice. McMahon had been everything. Not just confident, cocky. Not just good, great. Not just able to win games, but a winner. They were all qualities Young craved. He wanted to do the things McMahon had done on the football field. He just wasn't sure he could. Young was confident, good, and he had proven he could lead a team to wins. The question was, Could he take it to the next level? Could he replicate McMahon? In Young's mind, if he didn't duplicate what McMahon had done, he wouldn't be a success. Young convinced himself he *had* to live up to McMahon's standard.

As it turned out, Ted Tollner's stay in Provo was brief. After only one season, in February of 1982, Tollner left for a job with the University of Southern California.

Following Tollner out the door was defensive coordinator Fred Whittingham, a former teammate of Grit Young's when they were both playing for the Cougars. Whittingham had accepted a job with the NFL's Los Angeles Rams, meaning BYU would have a very different look in 1982, especially where it involved the quarterback. Not only would Young be taking over, but a new QB coach would be calling the shots. In that position, Edwards hired a little-known coach named Mike Holmgren from San Francisco State, whose main claim to fame was that he played quarterback for USC when O.J. Simpson was playing for the Trojans.

In the spring Blue-White game, Holmgren held out Young, with Gym Kimball and freshmen Blaine Fowler and Robbie Bosco taking most of the snaps. Kimball played very well. Unfortunately for him, the BYU coaching staff hesitated naming him the number-two quarterback behind Young. That was it for Kimball. If the coaches couldn't even pick him second-string outright, he wanted out. Kimball contacted Utah State, discovered the Aggies would welcome him with open arms, and that sealed the deal. Kimball bid farewell to BYU.

A few days after the spring game, Holmgren spoke about Young with the *Daily Universe*, BYU's campus paper. "Steve Young has great physical ability, an excellent arm, tremendous foot speed and running ability. He's an intelligent, intense young man, and I think all he needs to be a great player is a chance to be a great player."

Young's chance had arrived.

It's funny how things work out. Early in the 1980–81 school year, Young was contemplating quitting football altogether, leaving for a mission, or both. Young had even persuaded Keith Arbon, the roommate who wasn't so sure he wanted to go on a mission, to make the two-year commitment. Arbon was laboring in Perth, Australia, and Young would have to vicariously serve his mission through Arbon. For Young, there would be no two years away teaching complete strangers about Mormonism. His ascension up the depth chart had seen to that. Young's football future was now, and Nevada-Las Vegas was the first mountain to climb.

All-American center Bart Oates didn't seem the least bit worried about Young assuming control of the BYU offense. He told the *Universe*, "I really feel that by the time Steve graduates, he will be the best quarterback to ever play for BYU. Steve has a lot of intelligence when reading the various defenses, and he has 4.4 speed in the 40-yard dash, which makes him the running threat that McMahon wasn't." Apparently, the media covering the WAC felt much the same way. Before the season, they all cast votes predicting the conference's offensive player of the year. Young was the winner going away. They'd gotten used to watching one BYU quarterback after another assault the other WAC schools. The media didn't figure that would change just because McMahon was gone. For Young, all that was left was living up to the platitudes.

When Young was running the wishbone for the BYU junior varsity in 1980 against the UNLV JV team, the temperature at the Silver Bowl was 95 degrees. That would feel downright pleasant compared to what it was like the evening of September 2, 1982, when Young and the rest of the BYU players stepped onto the artificial turf of the Silver Bowl to open their season and the Steve Young Era. The thermometer read 108 when the game started, with the mercury shooting to 120 on the field.

Young hardly noticed. The heat was the least of the keyed-up, nervous quarterback's problems. All he wanted to do was make a better showing against the Rebels than he had in his last start as BYU's quarterback. It would also help if the defense would play a better game than the previous year when the Rebels upset BYU in Provo.

In Young's first start as BYU's unequivocal starter, things did come together. Young was workmanlike. The defense pitched a shutout and held UNLV to 160 yards of total offense. Young's numbers were good—not great—as the defense dominated the Rebels.

Young was glad to get the game over because a big game was on deck. The Cougars were on their way to Athens, Georgia, for a date with the Georgia Bulldogs. This game was similar to the Colorado game the previous year in that it would provide BYU with some national scope against a top-drawer opponent. Only Georgia was even more impressive than Colorado.

The Bulldogs had won the national title in 1980 and featured all-American running back Herschel Walker. Most everybody associated with the BYU program considered the Georgia game the most important in BYU football history.

To Larry Munson, Georgia's play-by-play broadcaster, BYU was just another non-conference opponent coming to Sanford Stadium for a big payday and an old-fashioned, southern butt-kicking. A couple of hours before the game, Munson asked *Salt Lake Tribune* beat writer Dick Rosetta to tape a segment for the Bulldogs' pre-game show. Munson hoped Rosetta could shed some light about BYU to Georgia fans. Munson's main interest was Steve Young, and how the junior quarterback would fare playing before 82,000 partisan fans and facing a swarming Bulldog defense. Rosetta had seen enough of Young and BYU football to feel confident predicting what Young would do.

"Do you see Young passing as much against the strong secondary of Georgia, especially if he gets picked off early?" Munson asked.

"If he's intercepted once or even a couple of times, he'll be right back firing at you again," Rosetta told Munson. "That's just BYU's offense. They keep coming at you."

Munson was skeptical. Of course, wide-open Western Athletic Conference football wasn't his forte. A team throwing 20 times in a game was a lot to Munson in 1982. He didn't realize that 20 *completions* in a half was not exactly front-page news to the BYU offense. Munson had watched Joe Namath, Ken Stabler, and Archie Manning do their things in the Southeastern Conference. But they were great passers in a conference that emphasized the run. Nothing could prepare Munson for a team that would throw the ball 40 or 50 times a game and think nothing of it.

At halftime, the score was tied at seven. BYU's defense had come to play, and it was anybody's game, amazing considering Young had thrown—count 'em— five interceptions. In McMahon's senior year, he had thrown only seven interceptions the entire season.

During a break in his halftime show, Munson left his booth in the Sanford Stadium press box and found Rosetta. "I guess they won't be passing as much in the second half," said Munson.

"You know what, Larry? They'll pass on the first play of the second half and they'll keep passing. You can bet on it."

In the locker room, Holmgren tried to get Young calmed down. Although Young had thrown the interceptions, only one had led to a Georgia touchdown, its only points of the half. Deflections had led to three of the picks. Holmgren explained that if Young could cut out the mistakes, BYU could still win the game.

Young came out passing in the second half. He threw 22 more passes, and hit wide receiver Scott Collie for a 21-yard scoring strike that gave BYU a 14-7 lead. Georgia scored a touchdown to tie the score again, and Kevin Butler hit a 44-yard field goal with 1:11 left in the game to give the Bulldogs the win. In a last-minute effort, Young threw his sixth interception. It had been an ugly performance, yet strangely, BYU was never out of the game.

On the charter flight back to Salt Lake City, the team was anything but despondent. The players knew they had scared Georgia; they just couldn't finish what they had begun. They hung with the number-six ranked Bulldogs, made a ton of mistakes, and almost came away with the win. Young's performance certainly wasn't satisfying, although he could take solace knowing he wouldn't face anything near that kind of talent once Western Athletic Conference play began. Young's only regret was that he couldn't generate more offense to coincide with the defense's big game.

"You're playing against guys who are twice as big and twice as fast. I think we weren't used to going against a defense with that much team speed," says Mike Eddo, a wide receiver on that team. "They had a lot of guys who were making plays. I don't think Steve threw any bad balls. His problem was he didn't have that much experience under his belt, and maybe not as much confidence then. I know he wasn't very happy with the way he played."

The Georgia game set the tone for what would turn out to be a very strange year. BYU had only lost three games the previous two years combined, so a BYU team losing a game, although not reason for panic, had been as rare as a LaVell Edwards smile. Before September ended, BYU would become better acquainted with losing, which would only add to Young's pressure in trying to maintain the high standard set by his predecessors.

With all of BYU's success in the '70s and early '80s, fan interest had risen to where Cougar Stadium could no longer accommodate all the people who wanted to see the Cougars play. Between the '81 and '82 seasons, construction workers did a makeover on the facility. Sixty-five-thousand seats now surrounded the Cougars' stage, and Young was playing the lead. Did anybody mention he was a nervous wreck?

The curtain-raiser at Cougar Stadium was not a memorable one. A party-like atmosphere prevailed at the game billed as the largest gathering for any sporting event in Utah's history.

Air Force was the team invited to join BYU in the opening of the stadium, and the Falcons were not hospitable visitors. The Cougars held a 38-31 lead when a coffin-corner punt pinned Air Force at its own one-yard line with 1:30 showing on the clock. For a wishbone team to go that far in such a short time seemed improbable. The Falcons proved it was not impossible. Quarterback Marty Louthan moved the Falcons up the field against a tired BYU defense, and all Young could do was watch in horror. Air Force eventually scored a touchdown, then sealed the win with a successful two-point conversion. It was a stunning loss. Young rushed 12 times for 97 yards and three touchdowns, and he was 19 for 28 for 215 yards passing with one passing TD.

This game turned out to be eerily reminiscent of the UNLV game in 1982 when Young was the fill-in starter. And Young took a lot of the heat from fans who called to talk about the loss with LaVell Edwards on his postgame show on KSL radio. Young had played very well, had directly accounted for four of BYU's five touchdowns, and put 38 points on the board. But fans whose afternoon had been ruined by the upset loss were roasting him. Welcome to the big-time, Steve.

Nobody really knew what to make of Steve Young after the Air Force game. As a starting quarterback, he had won two games and lost three. His stats were impressive enough. The results weren't. Maybe Scovil was right. Maybe Young didn't have what it took to be a major college quarterback. Maybe all the running Young was doing was messing up the fragile balance of BYU's vaunted passing offense. Many BYU receivers did become frustrated with Young's running. Young was still very immature at reading defenses, and when he could feel the pocket closing in on him, his tendency was to run instead of hanging in there and finding an open receiver. Many wondered if a running quarterback could flourish in BYU's system, especially since Sheide, Nielsen, Wilson, and McMahon had all been traditional pocket passers. Young's penchant for throwing interceptions was also alarming. There was conjecture that the phenomenal streak of BYU quarterbacks would end with Young doing his best impression of an Indy car crashing into the wall on the straightaway.

The week after the Air Force game, Young knew he had to do more. He couldn't become satisfied with his play. Edwards could see the pressure Young was feeling, and it became a season-long job for Edwards and Holmgren to get their young quarterback settled down. Young's friends tried to do the same thing.

Most of Young's close friends were teammates, and the little group he was a part of included kicker Lee Johnson, defensive end Jim Herrmann, tight end Gordon Hudson, and wide receiver Mike Eddo. There were others, of course, but that was the main group. They'd always find something to do with their time, but Young made sure he always worked hard at school. Whenever he called home, Grit's first questions had nothing to do with football. It was always questions about his classes. Young often told friends he couldn't get cocky or arrogant as BYU's quarterback because his dad wouldn't let him. Then again, neither would his friends.

Young and his friends worked hard at football, but they also knew how to have fun. Eddo was the new guy to the group, having transferred to BYU after playing at Saddleback Junior College. He had originally signed at the University of Illinois, but changed his mind after only a couple of days at the Champaign-Urbana campus. "It was kind of a party situation every night and I thought, If I keep this up I won't even want to play football anymore," says Eddo. Once he arrived at BYU, Eddo became friends with Glen Kozlowski, who had his wild side, and they found themselves in trouble with BYU's Honor Code which prohibited pre-marital sex, and the use of tobacco, alcohol, coffee, tea, and drugs. Not long afterward, Eddo hooked up with Young and his buddies.

He was the only non-Mormon of the group, which hardly mattered.

"When I went to BYU, I had no idea about the religion. I thought, Well, you can't drink coffee. It sounds so ridiculous, but I really had no idea," says Eddo. "I came from Saddleback where I was considered a goody-good. Then I got to Provo and some people thought I was kind of wild."

Eddo quickly learned Young and company's traditions. They'd pile into the Cardinal or Eddo's yellow Pinto, stop at the Brick Oven, a Provo restaurant, buy some cookies, then go back and crash at somebody's apartment and watch "Hawaii Five-0" reruns on TV while eating their cookies. They'd wash the cookies down with milk.

Only at BYU.

Hanging out with a group like this, guys with stronger personalities, allowed Young to be taciturn without anybody noticing or caring. Around these guys, he didn't need to be a leader. He could save that for the football field. That didn't mean they left Young alone. They knew he was uptight, which meant they had to relax him. They'd do it by giving him a bad time about any number of things. The Cardinal provided the group an unlimited source of material for showering grief on Young. There was also the way he dressed, both on and off the football field. That was one of the first things Eddo noticed about Young. He always wore jeans, t-shirts, and shoes with untied laces. In uniform, he was much the same. The style was for players to wear knee-high socks and pants that came to the knee. Young, doing his best Pete Maravich impression, wore stretched-out socks that barely reached past his ankle. He was a college junior and it looked like Young was wearing tube socks his mom had picked up for him in the seventh grade. Only these were tube socks that looked like they had been worn for a while, lost under the bed, then rediscovered a few months later.

The image of Steve Young was of a laid-back college student. On the outside he looked loose and relaxed. Inside, he was an ulcer waiting to happen.

Young needed some confidence-building games after losing two of the first three to open the season. He got them in Texas-El Paso and New Mexico. Who better to get well against than the Miners and the Lobos? The Cougars steamrolled past both teams, and quieted many of Young's critics as BYU improved to 3-2. Two more wins against Hawaii and Colorado State and BYU had some momentum.

In the Colorado State game, Young got the endorsement of Jim McMahon, who traveled to Provo during the National Football League players' strike to check out how his understudy was doing now that he was the starter. McMahon was still a revered figure at BYU. Consequently, Young held his mentor in the highest regard.

In the locker room after a tougher-than-expected win against the Rams, a team that picked off four Young passes, McMahon made his way to Young's locker where the two quarterbacks huddled for a few minutes. Young chatted up the Chicago Bear rookie, asking McMahon about specific situations and how he would have handled it. Still not totally comfortable in his role as starting quarterback, Young was looking for advice from any source.

He wouldn't get any words of wisdom from Krzmarzick. Like Jones, Haugo, and Kimball before him,

Krzmarzick decided his time had come. He notified Edwards that he was transferring to the University of Florida. With Krzmarzick's departure, only Young was left at BYU from the eight who were originally on that depth chart in the fall of 1980. With San Diego State looming on the schedule, Krzmarzick didn't want to face Doug Scovil and be reminded about what might have been had Scovil stayed at BYU.

Young, on the other hand, couldn't wait to play the Aztecs. He maintained in the days leading up to the San Diego State-BYU game in Provo that there was no revenge factor with Scovil, and that the game was just another conference affair the Cougars needed to win if they wanted to get back to the Holiday Bowl. It wasn't quite that simple. Young did want to play well. He wanted to prove to Scovil how misguided his assessment and treatment had been when he was a freshman. Maybe revenge didn't motivate him, since that wasn't in Young's nature. But Young's competitiveness and his burning desire drove him to prove to Scovil that he could play quarterback at BYU. Young very much wanted to beat a Doug Scovil-coached team. That was unequivocal, no matter what Young said to the contrary.

Young got his wish on November 13 when BYU cruised to an easy 58-8 win over San Diego State. It was a typical BYU laugher as Young passed for 284 yards on 22 of 35 passing. He threw one touchdown pass and ran for two more as part of a 94-yard rushing afternoon. When it was over, Young refused to say anything negative about Scovil, who didn't even go to midfield to shake Edwards' hand, let alone Young's. Scovil did complain about what he perceived as BYU running up the score, an ironic accusation since Scovil was famous at BYU for trying to score as many points as possible, no matter a game's margin or an opponent's feelings. Scovil also wasn't very generous in his praise of Young in his post-game comments. In fact, he didn't talk about Young's performance or mention him by name. Instead, Scovil focused his remarks on the BYU offensive line and the time they gave the quarterback.

"Doug knew Young was a great athlete and could run. But he didn't know exactly how good he was going to be as a college quarterback," says Dave Atkins, a Scovil assistant with the Aztecs, and later with the Philadelphia Eagles after Scovil was fired by San Diego State following the 1985 season. As it turned out, Atkins was one of the last people to see Scovil alive. Scovil suffered a heart attack and died at the Eagles' complex right before getting on an exercise bike during the 1989 football season.

After the win over the Aztecs, BYU went on to its ninth consecutive conference title and fifth straight appearance in the Holiday Bowl. The WAC named Young its offensive player of the year as selected by the conference's coaches and athletic directors, the seventh consecutive time a BYU signal caller had won that award. Young also achieved honorable mention all-American status from the Associated Press.

All the worry after the Georgia and Air Force games about whether Young would be a worthy successor to the throne reserved for BYU quarterbacks had been premature. What the postseason awards didn't provide was immunity from a loss in a bowl game. The 1982 BYU Cougars were a good team. The 1982 Ohio State Buckeyes were great.

BYU should have known it was in for a long night from the beginning. The Holiday Bowl game program cover drawing featured Young as a righthander. That was an omen of things to come. Young could have been ambidextrous for all the Buckeyes cared. Even today, LaVell Edwards says that the 1982 Ohio State team was one of the strongest he has faced as a BYU coach. After a slow start, the Buckeyes dominated the Cougars in the second half in the 47-17 win.

It was a very different Holiday Bowl for Young than his first in 1980 when he camped in front of a pinball machine. Back then, Jim McMahon was the story. In 1982, Young was. The Southern California press not familiar with Young's story scrutinized his every move. There was also a minor scandal when a Provo radio station called Lee Johnson in San Diego to talk about the game. The broadcaster asked Johnson where his roommate, Steve Young, was. Without missing a beat, Johnson said Young had broken curfew the night before and had been kicked off the team.

It was quite a lie, one that caused an apoplectic stir in Utah, where word traveled quickly. The rest of the day, Young had to refute Johnson's claim and calm everybody down. It was a typical Lee Johnson prank.

In their camp, the Buckeyes weren't doing much laughing. They wanted to be in the Rose Bowl, and they looked at the Holiday Bowl invitation as a consolation prize. One of those players who would have preferred a trip to Pasadena was Garcia Lane, who made sure Young wouldn't forget his encounter with the Buckeyes.

Lane, a junior defensive back, came on a corner blitz and nailed Young so hard it looked like he'd never get up. When Young finally did, he had a hurt hand and a spinning head. BYU put backup Blaine Fowler into the lineup for one play before Young came back on the field and took his customary place in the huddle. The problem was BYU's coaches hadn't sent Young back in; he just reinserted himself in the lineup. As Fowler was huddling up, Young tapped him on the shoulder and sent him back to the sidelines. Thinking Young was okay, the sophomore dutifully left the game. As it turned out, Young had a concussion and wasn't exactly thinking straight, and he didn't have the good sense to stay on the sidelines, a safe distance from the carnage. To become BYU's starting quarterback, Young had worked too hard. He wasn't in danger of losing his job, but he wasn't about to miss any action if he could help it. That episode typified Steve Young. He may have been a beaten man, but he was still going to be in there fighting.

CHAPTER SEVEN

One Phenomenal Season

S pring break was just beginning. A trio of Brigham Young University students were on their way to Scarsdale, New York, and Greenwich, Connecticut. Jill Simmons of Scarsdale, and Steve Young of Greenwich, were old friends. They had grown up together in the Mormon Church's Yorktown Stake, and it was Jill's father Ted who had gotten the recruiting ball rolling for Young and BYU when he contacted LaVell Edwards. With few Mormons in the area, the young people of the stake were a tight-knit bunch. Young and Simmons proved that. The third friend, Eric Hunn, a native of Shelley, Idaho, had never been to New York, so Young and Simmons invited him to join them on their adventure to the east coast.

Young had driven Simmons' brown 1980 Pontiac Phoenix all night on Interstate 80, with Hunn and Simmons sleeping most of the way. The Nebraska plains were flat, and the towns were small. It was a boring stretch of road with nothing interesting to see even in daylight. When they reached a decent-sized town, North Platte, Nebraska, Young decided to stop for breakfast. After the three ate, Young told Simmons and Hunn he was feeling good enough to keep driving, which he did for another hour before pulling over. It was approximately 10 A.M., Saturday, April 23, 1983. Hunn stayed in the back seat as Simmons took over the driving. Young moved to the front passenger side and quickly fell asleep. Eight minutes later, Young woke up and opened his eyes when he felt the car weaving. The car was drifting off the road, and Simmons was slumped against the door. Young quickly shook his friend, but she didn't respond. In fact, Simmons didn't even move. Young grabbed the wheel and tried desperately to get control of the car. It was too late. The Phoenix was careening off the road. Young braced himself as the car began to roll.

Amazingly Young and Hunn walked away from the wrecked car with only minor injuries. Young had a cut on his right wrist, and Hunn, a cut on his head. Simmons, the 19-year-old college student with such a bright future, was dead. Young and Hunn were both stunned.

The accident's investigating officer, Nebraska Highway Patrol trooper T.E. Ahrens, listed the driver's condition as "asleep" on the accident report, although Young had a different opinion. He had shaken Simmons and she hadn't moved. His shaking would have woken her, he presumed. The crash hadn't caused Simmons' death. Young was certain of that.

Curiously, no autopsy was performed, and Simmons' body was taken to Logan, Utah, for an April 27 funeral at the Logan Fifth and 18th LDS Ward Chapel. Following the accident, speculation about Simmons' health problems, specifically headaches that plagued her while she studied abroad in Israel during the fall semester of 1982, surfaced.

Were the headaches the actual cause of death? Did she have an aneurysm, as many people believed?

Young thought so, although he'd never know for sure. And it really didn't matter. One minute Jill Simmons was full of life; the next she was dead.

What had started as a simple spring break road trip had turned into a nightmare for Young. No football defeat could generate the emptiness he felt after Simmons' death. Young desperately needed something to go right. After Good Samaritan Hospital in Kearney, Nebraska, released Young, he was at a loss.

"It was just a tragedy," says Robbie Bosco, who moved up the depth chart as a freshman and sophomore and eventually replaced Young as BYU's quarterback in 1984. "I think the death was a very difficult thing for him. He didn't talk about it much, and it was just one of those things that you don't talk to a lot of people about."

So instead, the trauma of having a close friend die weighed heavily on Young's mind and left him wondering when or if things were going to turn around. He continued to feel the pressure that came with being BYU's quarterback. He attracted attention when he walked on campus. Church groups wanted him to speak at Mormon firesides, and complete strangers would stop him and want to talk. He began having a difficult time telling if people liked him for who he was or because he was BYU's quarterback. It was all stuff that came with being the big cheese at BYU. Young's personality and appearance suggested all was well. He didn't walk around after the accident in a haze, and he got on with life. Yet the death of Jill Simmons was something he was going to have to work through.

• • •

The main focus of Young's life was still football, and the 1983 season came with a lot of question marks. Young would be playing his final year behind five new offensive linemen, which was the most critical concern. Other key departures had left a lot of people wondering if the Cougars could maintain their streak of Western Athletic Conference titles and winning seasons. Predictably, many weren't convinced Young was cut from the same quarterback cloth as Sheide, Nielsen, Wilson, and McMahon. That may have explained why *Playboy*, in its 1983 college football preview, selected the Cougars to finish sixth in the conference and forecast a 5-6 season. What the magazine didn't explain was why it listed Ben Bennett (Duke), Wayne Peace (Florida), Boomer Esiason (Maryland), Chuck Long (Iowa), Doug Flutie (Boston College), Frank Seurer (Kansas), Jeff Hostetler (West Virginia), Tom Tunicliffe (Arizona), and Todd Dillon (Long Beach State) as the quarterbacks to watch in 1983, but not Young.

Todd Dillon? Tom Tunicliffe?

This was anything but the naked truth. The fact *Playboy* didn't exactly enjoy a high circulation in Provo, Utah, kept the outrage to a minimum, although it would have made for an interesting dilemma for buttoned-up Cougar fans had the magazine selected BYU to contend for a national title and for Young to win the Heisman.

Other preseason prognostications were much more generous in their assessment of the Cougars' and Young's chances in 1983. The reigning WAC Offensive Player of the Year, who finished second in total offense in 1982, was picked to defend his title by sportswriters and broadcasters who covered the WAC. LaVell Edwards also felt confident his quarterback could get the job done and eliminate some of the pressure he felt a year earlier.

At a gathering of Utah reporters at the Fort Douglas/Hidden Valley Country Club in Salt Lake City a month before the season began, Edwards said, "The pressure on Steve last year was unbelievable. He was wound up so tight three-fourths of the season because everyone was comparing him to McMahon. I had to tell him to forget that, that he was his own player, and to forget comparisons."

It was easy to say, tough to do.

Young spent a lot of time thinking about the pressure he had endured, both self-imposed and otherwise. He also pondered his first season as a Cougar starter. Was the team's performance an aberration? Could he lead the team the way McMahon had? Could the Cougars get back to double-digit victories and win a bowl game?

The onus fell squarely on Steve Young. Like all great BYU quarterbacks who had blazed the trail before him, Young had to be the leader. BYU had to be his team, and he had to be the guy teammates looked to for inspiration and confidence. Young wanted to assume that role, and the other BYU players voted Young one of the offensive captains. It seemed no matter where he went, being a team captain came with the territory.

Young was living with the Jim Burr family in the basement of their home on the east bench of Provo. As a freshman, Young had met Brett Burr, a walk-on, and they played on the junior varsity team together. The Burrs also had relatives who were members of the Yorktown Stake. When Jim and Carol Burr, parents of nine children of their own, invited Young and Lee Johnson to live with them, they didn't refuse. Young had always been a home-body, happiest when he could spend time with his family. The departure to BYU had left him homesick, and the Burrs' offer to move in with them helped fill that void. It gave Young a sense of family when his own was so far away. He always wanted to have a surrogate family to fall back on. He had that in the Burrs, and Young's buddies now had a gathering place.

"They were an unbelievably nice family. They'd go out of their way to treat you great and go the extra mile for you. You just knew they were genuinely nice people," says Mike Eddo, who moved into an apartment with Herrmann. "I don't really think it would have been good for Steve to live in some apartment complex. Even back then he was building up such a following. I think it was almost perfect for him to be able to live up on the hill and not down in the midst of all the students. Maybe that's why a lot of us went up there because it felt like you were kind of getting away from it, like you were getting away from school, and the football part of it. It was just a place to go and hang out."

And a place for Young to live.

Life was good. Young was doing well in school, he had enough money to put gas in The Cardinal, despite its gas-eating tendencies, he was playing a lot of golf, and there was the excitement of getting back on the field with a year's experience behind him and improving on what he'd done as a junior. Slowly, Young was beginning to enjoy himself.

When Young wasn't at the Burrs, it wasn't too hard to locate him. There was the Classic water slide on State Street. There was the Smith Fieldhouse where there was always pickup basketball being played. Another football player haunt was the Timpanogos Golf Course on the south end of Provo, the official site of golf games between Young and anybody else who wanted to play.

Young was a better golfer than most of his friends, but he wasn't as good as Robbie Bosco. "We would go out and play a best-ball and I would have to carry him," Bosco says. Young also wasn't as accomplished on the golf course as LaVell Edwards, and when the two would play Edwards would generally win. Young's 3.4 grade-point average proved he wasn't stupid. So did the fact he always "let" Edwards win when they played.

"There was nothing we ever did that wasn't competitive. We would go to the water slide all the time to see who could go down the fastest, who could get the highest on the bank, and all those things. It was a special group of people during those years and a very competitive group. Everybody wanted to outdo the other person," says Bosco.

Before the season, during two-a-day practices, Young, Hudson, Johnson, Herrmann, and Eddo would take off between sessions and sneak over to the water slide for a few laughs to alleviate the sometimes mundane nature of practice. Sneak was the operative word. Edwards and the rest of the coaches had no idea that the five players who all figured to play important roles in the Cougars' success were sneaking around behind their backs so they could go hell-bent-for-leather down a water slide.

"One time I hit Gordon Hudson so hard in the back coming down that I thought it was going to keep him out of practice," says Eddo. "I thought I was dead." To this day, Eddo is convinced Edwards never knew what they were up to.

As long as Young was still able to hit Eddo and Hudson on corner routes, and Herrmann was putting pressure on opposing quarterbacks, and Johnson was splitting the uprights and booming his punts, Edwards probably couldn't have cared less.

All five players got their first chance to do their things on the field in the season-opener against Baylor in Waco, Texas. Young and the rest of the offense looked at the game with the Bears with a lot of enthusiasm. It was another inter-sectional battle against a team from a conference, the Southwest, that was considered stronger than the WAC. There were more obvious reasons, too, especially to Young. Two of Baylor's four defensive backs were freshmen, and a third was a sophomore. Young figured to have a big game against Baylor's inexperience. He did.

Young threw one touchdown pass, ran for two others, rushed for 113 yards, and lit up Baylor for 351 yards through the air. The offense was going to be okay. That seemed obvious based on what BYU had done. The problem was the BYU defense, which couldn't stop Baylor. The Bears spoiled everything Young and the rest of the Cougars had been aiming for by coming away with a 40-36 victory. Young, who often felt the stinging words of angry fans after the losses the previous year, was off the hook in this one. The doubts this time were focused on a defense that gave up 40 points to a middle-of-the-road SWC team (87 points counting the Ohio State Holiday Bowl mishap).

"The loss to Baylor was bad. It was frustrating for us. We were moving the ball at will. It was a typical BYU defense where we had slow guys back there in the secondary and we're playing man-to-man defense against Gerald McNeil, the little receiver. They had two guys at receiver who ran 4.4 40s and we were back there playing man-to-man defense because we could not stop their running game," says Eddo.

On the charter flight from Waco, linebacker Todd Shell was livid. In preparation for the Baylor game, the BYU defensive coaches had the Cougars work extensively on a blitz package they felt would disrupt Baylor's platooning freshmen quarterbacks, Cody Carlson and Tom Muecke. But by game time, the conservative nature of BYU's defensive coaches had taken over and the blitz package was ignored.

"Can you believe our offense gave us 36 points and we can't win?" Shell asked rhetorically. He was speaking loud enough for the coaches to hear, and he didn't care. "This is unbelievable. We practice the blitz all fall then we come down here and we don't blitz one flippin' time. I can't believe it." Obviously, Shell was under enough control to insert the "flippin'" euphemism in place of a more popular adjective found on most other college football team charters. But it didn't mask how angry he really was.

As Shell continued to get a few things off of his chest, Young got out of his seat, walked over to the linebacker, and said, "Todd, don't worry about a thing. We won't lose another game the rest of the year."

Nothing could have fallen from Steve Young's lips at that moment that was more prophetic than his proclamation to Shell in the aisle of a plane cruising at 36,000 feet. Mormons believe Young's great-great-great grandfather was a prophet when he was leading the Mormon church in the 19th century. Maybe it was the pioneer stock coursing through Steve Young's veins. Who knows? Wherever his bold pronunciation originated from, it came true. The hot late-summer loss in Waco to the Baylor Bears would be the last time Steve Young tasted defeat while wearing the royal blue and white of BYU. The loss also marked the beginning of Young's unlikely march toward the Heisman Trophy.

The BYU sports information department had done its part by mailing a short video featuring Young and Hudson highlights to about 100 television stations in the country's major media markets. Sports Information Director Dave Schulthess was doing everything he could to get Young's name in front of the Heisman voters. Young would be responsible for the rest. When the season began, most "Heisman Watches" in newspapers didn't even list Young as a serious candidate. It wasn't a blatant omission like *Playboy*'s, but nobody figured Young was a legitimate aspirant. Ben Bennett was the quarterback most often listed as a potential winner, while running backs Mike Rozier of Nebraska and Oklahoma's Marcus Dupree were the early favorites. As the season progressed, with a lot of fanfare, Young's name began moving up in the unscientific polls while Bennett's dropped like so many incomplete passes.

Against Bowling Green in BYU's second game, Young decided he'd make sure he put a number on the board that would be enough to win. He riddled Bowling Green's defense for 362 passing yards, and directly accounted for seven of BYU's eight touchdowns. He threw for five and ran for two more in the 63-28 win.

Air Force was next, and Young continued to shine. Against the Falcons in Colorado Springs, Young completed an NCAA record 18 consecutive passes during one stretch, completed 39 of 49 passes overall, and hit for a career-high 486 yards as BYU piled up 725 yards of total offense in the 46-28 shellacking. These were numbers that could not be ignored. The nation was beginning to take notice and it wasn't just because of the great-great-great grandson angle. Young carried a 3.4 grade-point average in his double major of international relations and finance. Not surprisingly, he had been nominated for an NCAA post-graduate scholarship, and he openly talked about his desire to attend law school whether professional football opportunities presented themselves or not. Combine all that with his devout religious beliefs, his involvement with several different charitable organizations (he was the Utah State youth chairman of the American Cancer Society and the Utah Lung Association) *and* his football prowess and it was obvious why Young was a very popular man. The publicity would become more pronounced in the week preceding BYU's October 1 game. Steve Young and the rest of his BYU mates were going to Hollywood. UCLA was up next.

A game against UCLA in the Rose Bowl doubled the size of the normal press contingent covering BYU. The appearance of BYU also made reporters brush up on how many "greats" they needed to insert in their copy and scripts before they used the word "grandson" when writing and talking about Young.

The folks at CBS were hopping on the Young publicity train, and they made arrangements for Young to fly to Los Angeles a day before the rest of the team so he could tape an appearance on a CBS show called "Nightwatch." CNN also reserved Young for a Sunday morning interview after the UCLA game that would air later that evening. All Young wanted was for the CNN interview to come on the heels of a Cougar win.

The good part about the UCLA game was that another alphabet soup network, this time ESPN, would be televising the game live to its cable audience. ESPN in 1983 was not the monolith ESPN of 1995, but for BYU to have some national coverage, even if it was only cable, was welcomed.

UCLA, at 0-2-1, wasn't even a particularly good team at the time of its meeting with BYU. To the Cougars, it didn't matter. The Bruins were still the Bruins. In Young's one-plus years as BYU's starter, the Cougars had a propensity to win most of the games they were supposed to win. But they had trouble beating a quality, high-profile team. In 1982, they'd lost to Georgia and Air Force, both bowl-bound teams, and they'd been stomped in the Holiday Bowl against Ohio State.

For those reasons, although UCLA was winless and struggling, this was a game BYU had to have. For Young, the UCLA game would be his best chance to show Heisman voters that he was a legitimate quarterback, and it was also a chance for him to redeem himself after the bad showing down the coast in the Holiday Bowl ten months earlier.

In a half-full stadium, the game came down to the battle of Steves—BYU's Young and UCLA's Bono—another quarterback who was snubbed by *Playboy*. Bono wasn't even UCLA's starter at the beginning of the season. That honor belonged to Rick Neuheisel. But after the two losses and tie, Bruin coach Terry Donahue was looking for anything to change his team's fortunes. Bono, the less-celebrated Bruin QB, won the individual battle, com-

pleting the same amount of passes as Young (25) but
throwing for 129 more yards, 399 to 270 (the 399 yards
set a UCLA single-game record). Young also had three of
his passes picked off, while Bono was interception-free.
Yet Young was getting most of the accolades when the
final gun sounded because BYU had kept UCLA winless
with a hard-fought 37-35 triumph. Bono was the better
quarterback statistically that day, but Young found a way
for his team to win. It was an object lesson for Young to
see how players are perceived after losses and wins.
There's a lot more forgiveness, he figured out, if you
don't play well but your team wins. Young didn't play
well and he knew it. However, the next day in the papers, it was Young, not Bono, being showered with
praise. And the CNN interview Sunday morning after the
game was a whole lot of fun.

The toughest game on BYU's schedule was out of
the way; from then on it was a steady diet of Western
Athletic Conference teams. It almost seemed that as soon
as BYU got past UCLA, the Cougars put things in cruise
control because they made winning look painfully easy.

Against Wyoming, Young threw for 356 yards. Next
was New Mexico: four touchdowns, 359 yards. Then another game against Doug Scovil and San Diego State, another chance for Young to remind Scovil of his mistake:
446 yards passing, 51 yards rushing, three TD passes,
two rushing TDs. This time around, Scovil was a little
more generous in his praise of Young, saying, "Young
was great. I give him all the credit in the world."

The only bump in the road came against Utah State,
a team which hung a loss on the Cougars in 1982. The
annual Cougar-Aggie game would be no easier in '83, as
Young was knocked silly in the game's first series, but

continued playing before coaches became suspicious of his erratic, poor play and pulled him from the game. Dr. Brent Pratley, BYU's team physician, examined Young and diagnosed the star quarterback with a concussion. This time there would be no going behind the coaches' backs to get back into the game, as in his Holiday Bowl performance. Young was forced to wait for his head to clear, and for the doctor's okay before he was given clearance to go back and lead BYU to the last-minute 38-34 win. Trailing 34-31 with 50 seconds left, Young hit wideout Adam Haysbert for a 31-yard completion. Young then ran for 21 yards himself, and finally scored on a one-yard quarterback keeper with 11 seconds remaining as bedlam reigned in Cougar Stadium.

Physically, it was turning into a tough season for Young, who had suffered a deep thigh bruise against Wyoming and then the concussion against the Aggies. Young would be okay; Gordon Hudson and Mike Eddo would not. Hudson, the all-American tight end who was gunning for a second straight double-A honor, was lost for the season with a knee injury against Utah State. Eddo was also finished for the season with a broken clavicle. Young wasn't just losing two quality receivers, he was also going to have to play the rest of the season without two of his buddies.

None of this could stop Young, who was becoming a one-man publicity stop. By this time, everybody wanted a piece of him. *Sports Illustrated* had already been to Provo to do a Young-Hudson feature. Most of the major papers had either done something on Young or were planning to feature him before the end of the season. With this attention came the frequent requests for interviews. The ones in Provo weren't a problem.

The ones in New York were, at least to Mike Holmgren. BYU, which craved publicity and tried desperately to get Nielsen, Wilson, and McMahon on television without a lot of success, wasn't about to turn down chances for their bright light to extol the virtues of BYU while promoting himself and the football team. Like a good soldier, LaVell Edwards went along with it. So did Young. Holmgren, however, wasn't quite so understanding.

The week of the Colorado State game, Young flew to New York to tape several different segments with the networks. Before he left, Holmgren resigned himself to the inevitable. The quarterback coach was going to lose Young for at least two days because of travel, and at least half of another while Young was in New York. Holmgren was more than a little steamed at not having his quarterback at practice. It was fine that Robbie Bosco was getting experience working out with the first-team offense. But Holmgren worried about Young losing his sharpness due to lack of practice, and his worst fears were realized in the first half against Colorado State on November 13. BYU went scoreless in the first quarter, but scored on two Young TD passes for a 14-0 halftime lead. That wasn't good enough. Young hadn't been sharp, and Holmgren wasn't happy.

It had been a while since anybody got on Young hard about anything. Holmgren ended that streak in the locker room at halftime.

"You're playing horrible," Holmgren began, "and it's because you're never here to practice. When I was playing at USC, O.J. Simpson was on the team. O.J. Simpson. He went on to win the Heisman Trophy. And you know what? O.J. came to practice every day. He wasn't jetting off during the middle of the week skipping practice. He was there every day."

Young agreed with everything his coach was saying, although what wasn't to agree with? Young could tell the difference in his play when he practiced on a regular basis and when he didn't. He wanted to be at practice, but being pulled in so many directions it was hard. He just happened to be a great interview with a great story to tell. Truthfully, Young wasn't big on all the publicity. He'd have been just as happy hanging out with the guys in Provo as meeting with a bunch of talking heads for a two-minute sound bite. And it wasn't as if Young was skipping practice and going on vacation or sneaking away without consent. These weren't visits to the water slide. Everything he was doing was with LaVell Edwards' blessing. Young did what he was told, and if it meant flying to New York to meet with David Hartman on "Good Morning America," that's what he did.

During this stretch, the most glaring shortcoming in Young's game was in the pass efficiency department. He had achieved as high as a 170 rating only to see it plummet to 163 after the CSU game. Holmgren's message had been sent and Young got it. Boy, did he get it. Pity the University of Utah and the struggling Utes.

The final regular season game for both teams was set for November 19 in Provo. The Utes were their usual inconsistent selves, long since out of bowl consideration and playing mainly for pride, and, of course, the chance to beat BYU. The Cougars had far bigger fish to fry. They were rated ninth nationally, and had a shot at being ranked higher than any previous BYU team. All the publicity had paid off too. The Heisman field had been whittled to two contenders, Mike Rozier and Steve Young. Tom Tunicliffe's name was nowhere to be found.

Since Rozier played for football juggernaut Nebraska (he was its all-time leading rusher) and since the Cornhuskers were the nation's number-one-ranked club, the odds favored Rozier. Young had momentum on his side and he was the star of a very good team. Conventional wisdom said that wouldn't be enough for Young to become the first BYU quarterback to win the Heisman. It didn't mean Young had to quit trying.

The BYU-Utah game had unofficially become Steve Young Day in Cougar Stadium. Young's time at BYU had flown by. He was the first of BYU's great quarterbacks to not have redshirted. Everything he'd accomplished had come in four years total, but really in only two-plus years. A majority of BYU players would arrive at school, redshirt, go on a mission, then return. It wasn't abnormal to have a few seven-year guys on every BYU team. Young wasn't one of them. The one year of JV ball led to the one year backing up McMahon. Then it was baptism by fire in 1982, followed by the fairy tale that was his senior year.

Another reason for all the Young hoopla in his final home game was that Young was the kind of guy who went over well with BYU fans. He was handsome, humble, and happy, a player the boosters could idolize and feel good about. Young obeyed BYU's Honor Code, and he kept the Mormon Church's commandments. He was active in the church, and he performed service in his ward. He spoke at church firesides, he represented the university well, he signed autographs, and he even took special care to seek out little kids and sign for them. Once on Sports Central, a talk show on BYU flagship radio station KSL, Young was fielding calls from listeners. A girl, probably no older than 12, had an important question for Young and it didn't involve football.

"Steve, um, uh, do you have a girlfriend?"

"Well, how would *you* like to be my girlfriend?" he answered. The girl let out a small giggle, then probably began levitating. That was Steve Young. Essentially, he made people feel very, very good.

Against the Utes, a record crowd turned out to bid Young a fond farewell. There would be the Holiday Bowl in December, so it wasn't Young's swan song. It was, however, his final game in Cougar Stadium and it was against the Cougars' biggest rival.

Young didn't disappoint. He only threw for 268 yards, mainly because the BYU defense, which recovered two fumbles and had five interceptions, gave Young and the offense such good field position that the Cougars never had to go very far to get into the end zone. At halftime BYU led 35-7, and Young had four touchdown passes. He added two more scoring tosses in the third period before taking a bow and leaving the Cougar Stadium turf for the final time with less than a minute to play in the third quarter.

As Robbie Bosco trotted onto the field to replace Young, the sophomore quarterback congratulated his friend, put his arm around him, and raised Young's right arm in the air. Young patted Bosco on the shoulder, then he removed his helmet and let the cheers shower down on him. The final numbers were stunning. He completed 22 of 25 passes (88 percent) and threw for six touchdowns. The Cougars won 55-7. The normally reserved BYU fans stormed the field and brought down the goalposts, and Young's college career was almost over. For the entire fourth quarter, with the game long since decided, Young had mixed emotions. He'd known for a long time that his decision to go to BYU couldn't have been wiser. It was reaffirmed watching that final quarter from the sidelines in the party-like atmosphere. The only down side to the afternoon was when Bosco totally screwed up BYU's passing percentage by only completing 3 of his 4 passes in the one quarter he played.

The tradition at BYU is for each senior player to receive a blanket with the "Y" emblem at the last home game. Also by tradition, the stars of the team aren't saved and introduced last. Instead, each player is announced alphabetically. In what could only be described as fitting, Steve Young was the last player to receive his blanket. The name "Young, Steve" came after "Young, Jon," the Cougars' senior defensive back. Not surprisingly, the loudest cheer came when the last player's name was announced.

Young made his way to the locker room. As he did, he took time to accept congratulations from the many fans who were milling on the turf. Young didn't allow the emotion of the moment to really set in. In the south end of Cougar Stadium where BYU's locker room is located, there's a small room, a kind of holding tank, where LaVell Edwards meets with the press following games. This time, before Edwards' press conference began, Young took refuge in there and began crying. It was hitting him all at once. It was hard for Young to believe he'd never play another game in Cougar Stadium. The struggles he'd faced as a freshman had been as difficult as the last 11 games had been sweet. He'd endured it all and now felt worthy to take his place in the pantheon where great Cougar quarterbacks resided. During his trying junior season, Young used to ask himself if he'd ever be able to replace Jim McMahon. The new question was, Would Robbie Bosco be able to replace Steve Young?

• • •

Young had almost made good on the prediction he'd made to Todd Shell after the Baylor game. Only Missouri, BYU's opponent in the Holiday Bowl, stood in BYU's way. There would be a month to prepare, and Young would need all of it.

Almost immediately following the completion of the season, the awards began rolling in for both Young and Hudson. First, the Walter Camp Football Foundation named the duo to its all-American team. That distinction was followed by similar accolades from the Football Writers Association of America, Associated Press, United Press International, and the Kodak American Football Coaches Association. The quarterback and the tight end had run the board in the all-American business, becoming only the fourth and fifth Cougars respectively to garner consensus all-American honors.

Young was the national leader in total offense, averaging 395.1 yards per game (4,346 total), and passing efficiency. He completed more passes—306—than any player in college football history, he had 33 touchdown passes and only 10 interceptions, and his completion percentage of 71.3 also established a NCAA record.

In the classroom, Young's stellar GPA earned him academic all-American status. He was also one of 11 college football seniors honored by the National Football Foundation and Hall of Fame Scholar-Athletes. For his troubles, Young was given a $3,000 grant to pursue post-graduate work. The money had already been earmarked for law school tuition.

On November 29, Young and Hudson flew to New York for the Kodak announcement. On a visit to the Associated Press' main office in Manhattan, Young learned that his old buddy from Greenwich High, Mike Gasparino, had been named NCAA Division I-AA honorable mention all-American by the AP for his play at the University of Connecticut. Young returned to Provo on December 1, and two days later, was back on a plane headed for New York for the Heisman ceremony at the Downtown Athletic Club. Projections had Rozier winning by an easy margin. The speculation was that Young would finish second. That was okay with Young since it would make him the highest BYU Heisman finisher ever. Before leaving for New York, Young told friends he really didn't care if he won the Heisman or not. Those were his feelings *before* he arrived at the DAC. As Young walked into the club's lobby, the Heisman Trophy, the real deal, was on display. Young filed reverently past the hardware and touched it. It was at that moment that Young decided he really did want to win the award. He hoped his stats and BYU's success would carry enough weight to give him the upset win.

Nobody was surprised when Rozier was announced as the winner by a huge margin. Rozier captured 482 first-place votes to Young's second-best total of 153. Rozier's 1,801 total points easily outdistanced Young's 1,172. In a way, Young was relieved. Having been told all along that he had no chance to win, he hadn't prepared any remarks. He told friends later he would have felt awfully stupid standing before everybody with nothing to say.

A winner's speech, no matter how unprepared, was something Young should have been able to deliver. A month after the ceremony, it was revealed that Rozier had signed with an agent while still at Nebraska. By NCAA rules, this made Rozier a professional when he became the 48th winner of the Heisman Trophy. Rozier was not forced to relinquish the prize.

The two trips to New York were only the beginning of a hectic December. Young hung around the Big Apple for several days visiting his family before going back to Provo on December 8. On December 10, he jetted to Los Angeles for the taping of Bob Hope's Christmas show featuring the Associated Press all-American team. During one of the parties held in conjunction with the TV show, one of the players yelled, "Hey, Young, you want a beer?" As Young turned around to see who was doing the talking, someone else shouted back, "No, he's a Mormon. He doesn't drink."

The person answering for Young was Bob Hope.

Young made it back to Provo for four days of practice before heading back onto the road for a banquet at the Pigskin Club in Washington D.C. on Friday, December 17. That Sunday, the team departed for San Diego and the Holiday Bowl.

The ninth-ranked Cougars tried not to act too disappointed at having to play the Missouri Tigers, a team that had lost four games, with one loss to East Carolina at home, and one against Big Eight doormat Kansas. The Tigers had also shut out Oklahoma and beaten Illinois. The last and only other time BYU was ranked in the top 10 going into a bowl game was 1979, and that year the Cougars were upset they couldn't play a more worthy opponent than a fair Indiana team. The Hoosiers were so mediocre that they ended up beating BYU, 39-38. It was a similar scenario in 1983. On the other side of the field, Missouri wasn't in awe of BYU. The Tigers had faced the Big Eight's best. And they didn't see BYU as nearly as intimidating and good as Nebraska. It would make for an interesting battle.

One of the problems BYU always seemed to have in bowls was the loss of timing in its passing offense in the month between the end of the season and the bowl game. Utah's winters usually prevented BYU from holding any outdoor practices, and the only alternative was the open area in the Smith Fieldhouse where Ted Tollner had "discovered" Young. Only 40 yards long, it wasn't an ideal place to work on an intricate passing game. Another problem was that final exams always fell the week before the Holiday Bowl, killing much practice time before the team left for San Diego.

In the BYU offensive repertoire, gadget plays had never been very popular with LaVell Edwards. BYU would occasionally run a halfback pass, and an end-around or double reverse would be pulled from mothballs a couple of times a season. It wasn't so much that Edwards disliked the flea-flicker as much as BYU seemed to have no trouble moving the ball and keeping defenses on their heels by simply passing the football. Each year, though, the trick plays would make it into the BYU package, and occasionally they would make an appearance during a game.

In the sixth annual Holiday Bowl, the Cougars played the game straight up for most of the evening in San Diego, and a fat lot of good it did them. They'd drilled teams all season, but when it came time to strut their stuff, the offense seized up. Young was a mere 9 for 17 with three interceptions in the first half. The 1983 season, Steve Young's personal fairy tale, looked like it would have a Stephen King ending. BYU was struggling to score and struggling to stop the bigger, faster Tigers. Missouri was hanging onto a 17-14 lead when it gave the ball back to the Cougars 93 yards from the end zone with only 4:13 remaining in the game.

Young had been brilliant in the second half. He'd righted the ship. He just couldn't get the offense into the end zone with any regularity. Down three, the Cougars needed to score. In the huddle as the offense returned to the field, things were very calm. Young and the other 10 players understood the task. All they had to do was execute.

After a first down and a sack of Young, the sixth of the game, Young was on the run again, almost being sacked by Taft Sales at the BYU five. Young somehow got away and found Mike Eddo wide open for a 53-yard completion that gave the Cougars hope. Three plays later, Young fumbled the ball, and when it looked like Missouri was going to snuff out BYU's final drive, the Cougars somehow recovered. That play set up a fourth-and-the season play. A Young to Waymon Hamilton pass barely got BYU the first down. That set up a play which cemented Steve Young's place in BYU football lore.

BYU receivers coach Norm Chow, who called BYU's plays from the press box, named the play Fake Right 28, QB Screen Left. The play was in the Holiday Bowl gameplan, it just wasn't up there with, say, the draw trap, a wide receiver corner route, or a 10-yard out pattern.

The play called for the running back to take a handoff from the quarterback, and run a sweep to the right. As the running back ran, he was supposed to stop and look for the quarterback in the flat away from the play. The running back would throw the ball, the quarterback would catch it, and run until he couldn't run anymore. That's the way it was drawn up in the playbook and that's the way BYU practiced it on the rare occasions the Cougars did work on it. Sometimes it worked and sometimes it didn't.

Thirty seconds were left on the clock when Chow sent in the play. He'd noticed the cornerbacks cheating up, and he thought he could exploit that. Young called the play. The running back/passer on the play would be Eddie Stinnett, a big, strong runner who had completed a touchdown pass earlier in the season. The quarterback/receiver, of course, was Young. It was third and one, and BYU was going to spring a surprise.

As the play unfolded, it looked like a normal sweep to the right until Stinnett stopped and set to throw. As he did, Sales, the Mizzou linebacker, saw the play coming and ran toward Young with the idea of either intercepting or batting the ball. Sales did neither. He was a half-step late as he tried in vain to knock the ball away. Instead, Stinnett's rainbow cleared Sales' outstretched arm and made its way to Young, who caught the bottom half of the ball and somehow hung on. In the end zone, Adam Haysbert made a key block.

When Steve Young was named quarterback at BYU, many people questioned his ability to throw the ball. Many suggested Young was only a good runner. During his four years at BYU, Young spent almost all his time trying to perfect his throwing motion and improve his accuracy as a passer. As Young said once, "Anybody can run. How many guys do you know who practice running?"

It's ironic that Young's sheer athletic ability would carry BYU through on this play. Young's missiles had gotten the Cougars to this point. It was now time for a run. With a path to the end zone, Young made a move against the grain with one goal in mind—the goal line.

When the normally reserved Young crossed into the end zone, he did the same thing that thousands of Cougar fans were doing in the aisles of Jack Murphy Stadium and in their living rooms in Utah. He danced. Young bounced from the turf and began running around like a little kid. He only stopped when wide receiver Kirk Pendleton reached him and began hugging him. The look of exhilaration on Young's face said it all. The Cougars had won in the most unlikely fashion with Young, the all-American boy, playing the hero. It was his first and only catch as a collegian. The finish was almost hokey, and maudlin, and so, well, Hollywood.

Unless you'd seen it, you wouldn't have believed it. The play, that is. Of course you could say the same thing about Steve Young's senior season.

CHAPTER EIGHT

The $40 Million Man

J. William Oldenburg was loving life and living large. Very large. The president of Investment Mortgage International Inc., had an announcement to make. It was a gala atmosphere on December 22, 1983, and not because Christmas was three days away. This was big. Oldenburg was not about to issue a simple press release declaring to the free world that he was purchasing the United States Football League's Los Angeles Express from cable television mogul Bill Daniels and his partner Alan Harmon. No, Oldenburg would announce this business deal at the opulent Beverly Hills Hotel. He would have it no other way. Loud, ostentatious, overblown. That described the press conference. It also describes Bill Oldenburg.

Wayne Newton, Oldenburg's best friend, flew in from Las Vegas for the press conference, and was introduced as a member of the Express' new board of directors. Mercifully, Newton didn't sing. For whatever reason, Oldenburg also invited his friend, that internationally recognized football fan, Orson Welles, to the festivities.

Once the champagne and hors d'oeuvres were gone and the celebrities had departed, what Oldenburg had for what he said was a $7 million sale price but turned out to be only $4.9 million was a team that had won eight and lost 10 the previous year, averaged only 19,000 fans (an exaggerated number) per game in the spacious 92,000-seat Los Angeles Coliseum, and lost for Daniels and Harmon somewhere in the vicinity of $3 million to $4 million. Oldenburg had just added to his portfolio a team without any marketable, name players. That, Oldenburg decided, would soon change.

Down the California coast in San Diego, Steve Young and the rest of his Brigham Young teammates were preparing for the Holiday Bowl in Jack Murphy Stadium against Missouri. Young had one thing on his mind, finish the 1983 season—one of the finest turned in by a quarterback in college football history—with a flourish.

Throughout his senior season at BYU, Young pointed to the National Football League draft scheduled for May 1. He hadn't ruled out the USFL; he just didn't have the new league at the top of his list. During Young's senior season, George Curtis, the Express' head trainer, traveled to Provo on several different occasions to watch some BYU games and do informal scouting for the team. He was also on a fact-finding mission. Curtis, a Mormon whose wife was from Utah, knew BYU coach LaVell Edwards, and was well acquainted with the Cougar football program. Curtis also knew Steve Young, which led to the two occasionally speaking about the Express and the USFL.

"Would you be interested in the USFL, or are you one of the guys who says he's only going to play in the NFL?" Curtis asked Young one day.

"No, I'd talk to them," Young replied.

That's all Curtis needed to hear.

The Los Angeles Express were selecting 11th in the first round of the 1984 USFL draft, and Bill Oldenburg was anxious to play with his new toy. He wanted a quarterback, and he already had in mind who that quarterback was going to be. The year before, the Express had drafted the nation's most celebrated college quarterback, the University of Pittsburgh's Dan Marino, and they even flew him to Los Angeles for a press conference. Marino, however, signed a contract with the NFL's Miami Dolphins. This time Oldenburg was calling the shots, and he had Steve Young in his crosshairs. He wasn't about to let the top quarterback get away from the Express again.

Oldenburg knew Young would be long gone by the 11th pick of the first round. That didn't sit well with the owner who desperately wanted to be in position to pick the BYU all-American. Also, Oldenburg didn't want to give up anything to get a shot at Young, who probably would be one of the first three players selected. Then Oldenburg had an idea, and he prevailed on his fellow owners for their cooperation. He asked his USFL brethren to skip over Young on their turns to draft, reasoning that the team in the second-largest television market in the league needed a marquee player. For the good of the league, the other owners agreed to leave Young alone. Oldenburg's wheeling and dealing had paid off. Steve Young was his to sign or lose.

All the pieces were falling into place. It was now Don Klosterman's turn to make the draft a success. There was no better guy to run the Express' football operations than Don Klosterman. The Duke (Klosterman's nickname) knew a thing or two about quarterbacks and upstart football leagues. After all, Klosterman had been a hotshot college quarterback himself at Loyola University, and had gone on to be a number-one draft pick of the Cleveland Browns. A skiing accident cut short his playing career, so Klosterman rattled around for a while selling insurance before taking a front-office job with the Los Angeles Chargers of the American Football League. After the Chargers moved to San Diego, Klosterman signed Lance Alworth, Ron Mix, Keith Lincoln, and John Hadl, and built a league power while building his own resume. Klosterman then performed similar reclamation projects with the Dallas Texans and the Houston Oilers before finally going to the NFL's Baltimore Colts, and eventually the Los Angeles Rams. It was from the Rams that Oldenburg plucked Klosterman to head the Express' football operations and assemble talent that would turn an 8-10 team under Bill Daniels and Alan Harmon into a championship contender.

Eight days after taking over as the Express' general manager, Klosterman called his old buddy from his San Diego days, John Hadl, to gauge Hadl's interest in coaching the Express. Hugh Campbell, an amazingly successful Canadian Football League coach who had coached the Express in their inaugural season, hadn't found the USFL to his liking and bolted to the NFL and the Houston Oilers after one season. Klosterman had one man in mind to replace Campbell, and that man was Hadl. It was Klosterman who had signed Hadl to his first pro contract in 1961, and now he was courting Hadl again. Hadl, who was living in his hometown of Lawrence, Kansas, after assistant coaching stints with his alma mater, the University of Kansas, and with the NFL's Denver Broncos, caught a flight to Las Vegas for a job interview. No other candidates were even being considered. It was Hadl's job if he wanted it. Klosterman told Hadl his plan was to build the Express with rookies, and, in fact, put together the best young football team in history. Klosterman's track record and Oldenburg's seemingly deep pockets convinced Hadl. He was moving to California to take his first head coaching job.

A few weeks before the draft, Curtis, the Express trainer, met with Klosterman and told him the Express could improve their chances of signing Steve Young if they drafted Gordon Hudson and signed him first. If Hudson, the BYU tight end and Young's favorite receiver and close friend, was to sign with the Express, it would greatly enhance the Express' likelihood of nailing down Young, Curtis explained.

On January 4, the morning of the USFL draft, Klosterman, Hadl, and Curtis—still the trainer, but more importantly, the team's Steve Young liaison—convened at 7 A.M. in Klosterman's office at the Express' Manhattan Beach headquarters to discuss the draft. Everything was in place, and Klosterman and Hadl, after discussions with Oldenburg, knew what they wanted to do with their picks. This meeting was to see if drafting Young was feasible.

"You told us that Steve Young would be interested in signing a USFL contract if all the situations were correct. Is that right?" Klosterman asked Curtis.

"Yes, sir. That's what he told me," Curtis replied.

"We just talked to Mr. Oldenburg, and he's extremely interested in pursuing Steve Young as a draft choice. But it'd be a waste to draft him if he won't sign. Is there any way you can get Steve Young on the phone?" Klosterman said to Curtis.

"I can try."

Curtis found the number for the BYU football office in Provo and called his friend Shirley Johnson,
BYU's football secretary. Johnson told Curtis that Young
was in Hawaii for the Hula Bowl, and that he wasn't
available.

"Do you know how to reach him in Hawaii? I need
to talk to him."

"Do you know what time it is there?" Johnson said.

"It doesn't matter what time it is. I'm talking about
his future. If I don't get a hold of him, the Los Angeles
Express aren't going to draft him."

Johnson tracked down the name of the hotel where
Young was staying, and gave Curtis the number. It was a
little after 4 A.M. Hawaii time when the phone in Young's
hotel room rang. Young was groggy when he answered.

"Steve, this is George Curtis. Can I talk to you?"

"George, do you know what time it is?"

"Yeah, I do. Hey, there was a story going around
that you don't want to play in the USFL, and that you
would only sign an NFL contract. Is that true?"

"No, that's not true."

"Steve, I'm sitting here with Don Klosterman and
John Hadl. Let me give the phone to them, you tell them
the same thing you told me, and we'll see what happens
when the draft starts in the next hour."

Curtis gave way to Klosterman, who talked to
Young for about five minutes. The Express' president
and general manager then gave the phone to Hadl, and
he spoke to Young for a few more minutes. Both
Klosterman and Hadl were smiling as they confirmed
what Curtis already had told them. If the situation, the

money, the contract, all the things that go into signing a player, were right, Young would be interested.

Later that day, the Los Angeles Express notified Steve Young they had drafted him.

Having spent his teenage years near New York, Steve Young had grown up a fan of the New York Giants, and he idolized Dallas Cowboy quarterback Roger Staubach. Young had always dreamed of playing professional football, that is, National Football League football. During their Greenwich High days together, Willie Atkins used to joke with Young that one day Atkins would play for the New York Knicks and Young would play for the Giants. That sounded good to Young. He could see himself eluding would-be tacklers and throwing for touchdown after touchdown. Those were the dreams of two teenagers, not unlike the dreams of any boy who had ever played sports. Now, the signal caller had guaranteed he would get the chance to play football for a living. Pro scouts had been hounding him since his junior year, and speculation had Young headed to the Cincinnati Bengals. The Bengals were holders of the NFL draft's first pick, and they were making overtures that Young would be their selection. The only problem was, the Los Angeles Express had struck first.

Further complicating the matter for Cincinnati was the issue of the Bengals' current starting quarterback, Ken Anderson. Anderson had led the Bengals to Super Bowl XVI, and though a veteran, he was still firmly entrenched as Cincinnati's number-one QB. The thought of holding a clipboard as Anderson's backup for two, three, maybe four years before he would get his shot was not attractive to Steve Young. First and foremost, Young wanted to play, and it didn't look like he'd have that chance in the immediate future with the Bengals. He would, however, with the Express, and soon. The United States Football League's second season was set to begin the last week of February. There would be a lot for Young to consider over the next two months.

Following his selection by the Express, Young hired attorney and sports agent Leigh Steinberg to represent him, and the two men began to study Young's options. The Cincinnati Bengals had many player personnel problems, and many holes to fill. The legendary Paul Brown, who had guided the Bengals as an expansion franchise and built them from the ground up only to watch them plummet into the abyss by 1983, wasn't sure he could afford not to select with the first pick a player who could possibly turn out to be the franchise's quarterback of the future. Cincinnati, in casual conversations with the media, would not make a firm commitment as to its intentions with the top pick. It quickly became a "Will they? Won't they?" scenario that Klosterman felt he could play to his advantage. Klosterman wasn't about to wait for Cincinnati. He had already laid the foundation to get Young, and now he was ready to make his moves.

Klosterman hired Sid Gillman as an Express assistant coach and football consultant. In 1983, Gillman was the general manager of the Oklahoma Outlaws before a falling out with higher-ups hastened his retirement. Klosterman was bringing the 72-year-old Gillman out of mothballs. Gillman's honorary title in football circles was a simple one: The Father of the Forward Pass. Gillman devotees called him the best football coach ever. Gillman had been Hadl's head coach when Hadl was a player with the Chargers. In Hadl, the Express had a coach who had thrown for more than 33,000 yards during a 16-year professional playing career, and complementing him as an assistant coach was the respected Gillman. To persuade Steve Young to spurn the NFL and sign with the Express was a conundrum that Klosterman had to solve. But with Hadl and Gillman on board, coaches who espoused the passing game, two of the puzzle pieces were in place. More pieces were quickly added. On January 17, Bob Rose, the Express media relations director, sent out a press release announcing the team had signed eight players to contracts. Of the eight, one name stuck out more than the others. Los Angeles heeded Curtis' advice, and signed tight end Gordon Hudson to a contract. The Hudson signing was a calculated risk by Los Angeles. Hudson's pro stock had dropped considerably when he went down with the knee injury during his senior year at BYU. Klosterman and Hadl both understood there was no way Hudson would play at all in the 1984 USFL season. Of course that wasn't the reason they'd drafted Hudson. The big tight end, they felt, was their ticket to Steve Young. With Hudson under contract it gave Young another reason to sign with the Express—the chance for the duo to pick up where they left off at BYU, the star quarterback throwing to the star tight end.

All of Klosterman's moves to this point had been for one purpose. As an AFL man at heart, Klosterman knew the impact Joe Namath had on the league when the Alabama quarterback signed with the AFL's New York Jets. Namath's signing had given the league instant credibility. Then when Namath's Jets defeated the NFL's Baltimore Colts in Super Bowl III, a legend was born. To say Steve Young could have a similar effect on the fledgling USFL was, at least in Don Klosterman's mind, a legitimate presumption. The USFL's New Jersey Generals had signed Georgia running back Herschel Walker, and the Pittsburgh Maulers had 1983 Heisman Trophy winner Mike Rozier under contract. Logically, it was the Express' turn to nail down a superstar.

The Duke's next move was a cannon shot that landed a direct hit on the bow of the NFL's ship. Less than two weeks before the USFL season-opener, the Express announced they had signed Baylor's Mark Adickes, Oregon's Gary Zimmerman, and Texas' Mike Ruether to contracts. Not coincidentally, the three players were considered the best offensive linemen available in the draft. For good measure, Klosterman also inked Jeff Hart to an Express contract. Hart had started on the Baltimore Colts' offensive line in 1983, and was a proven player.

The signing of the offensive linemen was ostensibly a move to lure Young to Los Angeles. The strategy was also vintage Don Klosterman. As a football man, Klosterman felt the best way to build a football team was with strong, young offensive linemen. That was the Duke's theory in the AFL and the NFL. He wouldn't deviate from that in the USFL. The immediate impact of a strong offensive line would be the quarterback being kept from getting knocked on his rear. It was also the way Klosterman wanted to build the Los Angeles Express.

Klosterman signed each of the offensive linemen, but it wasn't easy. For a successful businessman, Oldenburg didn't seem too savvy when it came to negotiating with players. When the Express were courting Adickes, Oldenburg, in front of Adickes' agent and Klosterman said, "I like this kid. Give him whatever he wants."

So much for bargaining power. Oldenburg's spontaneous bursts of generosity and idiocy hamstrung the Duke, but then, it wasn't Klosterman's money. If

Oldenburg wanted to throw it around, that was the way it would be. Klosterman was just elated to have the players under contract. In his mind everything was in place. The Express had offensive-minded coaches, a close friend as a receiver, and guaranteed solid protection on the playing field, all things they hoped would convince Steve Young to play for the Express. The Duke finally had his sales pitch, and was ready to knock on Young's door and present a demonstration of his product. He'd done his part. Now it was Oldenburg's turn. The former bank clerk from Syracuse, New York, had to put a financial package together that Young could not refuse. Oldenburg gave that responsibility to Martin Mandel, Investment Mortgage International's corporate attorney.

• • •

The wheels began turning when the two groups, Leigh Steinberg representing Young, and Mandel, negotiating on behalf of Bill Oldenburg and the Los Angeles Express, initiated informal discussions. Obviously, Young had bargaining power. The negotiations were in their infancy, and the first game of the USFL's regular season was set for February 28. Eight days had passed since the four offensive linemen had joined Los Angeles, and negotiations quickly got serious. Oldenburg invited Young and Steinberg to IMI's corporate headquarters at 101 California Street in San Francisco for a sit-down visit on Tuesday, February 21. If people thought the press conference to announce Oldenburg as the Express' new owner was lavish, they obviously hadn't been in IMI's offices.

"Some would call them opulent, some would call them garish. They were magnificent," says Mandel of the offices where he worked. The 43rd-floor suite, along with the 41st and 42nd floors, rented for a cool $280,893 per month. The offices had floors made of marble imported from Italy, rosewood-paneled walls from Brazil ("I hate to think in this era of political correctness how many rosewood trees died for all of the rosewood paneling," adds Mandel), and sculptures and art work all over the place. It was like a museum. There were red velvet Chippendale-style arm chairs, mahogany dining room tables, and walls that opened automatically, revealing television sets. A spiral staircase connected the floors, providing access to the gymnasium, complete with jacuzzi and workout equipment. The offices also had a private dining room and bar.

As Young and Steinberg entered through voice-activated doors, they immediately noticed a curious gong with Chinese characters on it that stood as the office's centerpiece. Young later learned that an employee would ring the gong whenever a million-dollar deal was signed for IMI. This was the kind of wealth Young grew up around in Greenwich. It was the kind of wealth that never impressed him.

As Young looked up, he noticed the message board in the lobby that ordinarily detailed the day's stock quotes. This day it said: STEVE YOUNG, MR. BYU, MR. UTAH, MR. EVERYTHING. It all seemed a little much. Give Oldenburg credit, though. He went all out.

In trying to determine how much money the Express should offer Young, Mandel tried to establish some parameters. In May of 1983, Stanford quarterback John Elway signed a series of five one-year contracts with the Denver Broncos for $1 million per year. That same year, Edmonton Eskimo quarterback Warren Moon jumped from the Canadian Football League to the NFL and signed with the Houston Oilers. Mandel reasoned that Young should be paid equally, or at least be somewhere in that ballpark.

Mandel then attempted to spice up the deal a little. He talked to some pension and financial consultants who helped him add some things to the contract that would entice Young. "We structured the deal to make Steve the highest-paid athlete on the basis of a gross-dollar contract. We also structured the deal so that anybody looking at it from an actuarial standpoint could see that in real dollars, Steve was being well compensated," adds Mandel.

As the two sides met, Oldenburg put the Express' offer on the table. The contract called for a lot of money up front, with the rest of it deferred for several decades. Oldenburg gave Steinberg and Young until February 24 to look the numbers over. Steinberg agreed, and in turn began dialogue with the Bengals. The attorney went to the Bengals armed with plenty of questions. Were they planning to draft Young? Would they trade the first pick? What kind of money would they offer? Guaranteed? What kind of signing bonus? None of Cincinnati's responses were particularly appealing to Steinberg. The Bengals had a reputation for being cheap by NFL standards, and Paul Brown was definitely old school. Reports had Cincinnati prepared to offer Young a five-year, $2.5 million contract, with only part of the money guaranteed. Others bumped that figure to $3.5 million over the same period. Whatever, it would have made Young the highest-paid Bengal in team history. For Cincinnati, it was extremely generous. The Bengals were also ready to reward Young with a signing bonus of about $1 million. Not bad, but not close to the Express' offer. If what Oldenburg had proposed was an Italian marble-floor, the terms of the Bengals' proposal was linoleum from Akron.

Even with the talk of big—really big—money swirling around, these were not good times for Young. The thought of becoming an instant millionaire wasn't that appealing to a guy who still drove a '65 Oldsmobile and did most of his dining at Burger King. The whole negoti-ating process had been overwhelming, and Young found himself vacillating between the NFL and the USFL, the Bengals and the Express. Young was still unsure of what he was going to do. On Friday morning, March 2, while Young prepared to fly via private plane to San Francisco for another round of talks, his phone rang. On the line was Roger Staubach, the same guy whose poster had hung in Young's bedroom on Split Timber Place for all those years. *The* Roger Staubach was calling Young and suggesting he strongly consider the NFL over the money of the USFL. The two spoke about stability, tradition, and money during the ten minutes they were on the phone together. Staubach, clearly a hired gun dispatched by the NFL to talk to Young, was nonetheless sincere in his feel-ings for the league. He felt Young would be better served by toiling in the NFL, and he said as much. Young was thrilled that Staubach would take time to call him, and a lot of the things the former Heisman Trophy winner said made sense. It was one more thing for Young to think about as he drove to the Provo airport for his flight to California.

His first night in San Francisco, Young didn't sleep much. He wanted to take things slowly, and Oldenburg didn't. The pressures of the negotiations showed in the early hours of March 3. Steinberg had reservations about how much money Young would get up front, and he was also concerned about the deferred-payment plan: how much and for how long. Steinberg felt they were valid points. Oldenburg was incredulous. He was offering fairy-tale kind of money, and Steinberg and Young were stuck on details. Oldenburg, a simmering teapot most of the night, began whistling. Angrily he poked Young in the chest and yelled, "You're never going to make more money than this." He took some cash from his wallet and tossed it at Young.

Young pushed Oldenburg's hand away and told him he'd be wise not to touch him again. An infuriated Oldenburg hastily called off the negotiations and asked Young and Steinberg to leave. In Greenwich, LeGrande and Sherry Young were poised to make the cross-country flight to California for what they thought was going to be the contract signing. When Oldenburg's outburst occurred, Steve called his folks and told them to stay put. The decision had been put on hold.

Panicked by this turn of events, Klosterman began damage control. He had known Steinberg for quite some time, and it was his and Mandel's job to bring the two parties back together. "That was the one night when none of us thought the deal was going to happen," says Mandel. "Bill was a somewhat mercurial personality. So the main goal was to remove him from negotiations to allow the deal to get done. That was my job for the L.A. Express in any number of the football agreements that I negotiated."

Two days later, after feelings had been assuaged, Young and Steinberg flew to Los Angeles, where they were whisked by limousine to Klosterman's house in the Hollywood Hills, where they would join Klosterman's other guests, Bill Oldenburg and Mandel. The limousine was only slightly larger than Young's '65 Oldsmobile, but considerably cleaner. At Klosterman's house, another bargaining session ensued, and this meeting went much better. The men dined together while trying to patch things up. A verbal agreement was reached, and the next day, in Oldenburg's private box at the Los Angeles Coliseum, while Oldenburg and Steinberg watched the Express lose to the Birmingham Stallions, 21-14, before a crowd of about 10,000, all the details were worked out. The Express' record dropped to 0-2, and the team looked more than a little ragged. But that didn't matter. Mandel and Steinberg had done their jobs, and Oldenburg had gotten his man. Steve Young was the newest member of the Los Angeles Express.

After the loss to Birmingham, Express quarterback Frank Seurer, who had replaced an ineffective Tom Ramsey in the third quarter of the loss to Birmingham, was told by Hadl that he would start the following week's game against the Oakland Invaders. Feeling good about the turn of events, Seurer left the locker room and was greeted by a man who escorted him to the owner's limousine outside the stadium.

"Mr. Oldenburg would like to talk to you," the burly man said. Inside the limo was Oldenburg and his daughter. Seurer had only met the owner a couple of times previously, and hadn't had so much as a conversation with Oldenburg. In the spacious back seat, Oldenburg began tossing accolades at Seurer, telling him how well he played, what a great quarterback he was, and how bright his future was with the Express. Seurer knew Oldenburg had been drinking, yet he was still flattered by the attention. Later that night, Seurer heard that the

Ever since his college days, Young has been a popular banquet speaker. (*Daily Universe*)

For most of the 1982 season, Cougar fans weren't sure Young was the next great BYU quarterback. His performance in 1983 removed all doubts about his abilities. (*Daily Universe*)

Young's ability to leave the pocket and run gave the BYU offense a weapon it had never enjoyed before. (*Daily Universe*)

There were a few anxious moments leading up to the 1983 Heisman Trophy announcement, although Young wasn't surprised when Nebraska running back Mike Rozier walked away with the hardware. (Courtesy of the Downtown Athletic Club of New York City, Inc.)

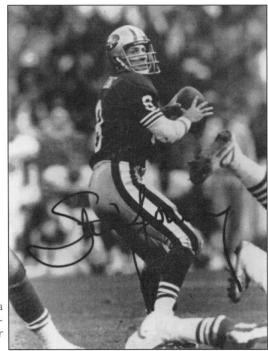

The left-handed Young has a style that bears little resemblance to Joe Montana, his 49er predecessor. (*Daily Universe*)

Young opened the 1982 BYU season with an efficient performance against the University of Nevada, Las Vegas. (*Daily Universe*)

With a Super Bowl title tucked safely away, Young has plenty of reasons to smile.

Despite his gaudy statistics, Young always had to overcome the rap of being a player who couldn't win the big game. His 1994 season silenced his critics.

Young handles thousands of autograph requests every year.

Steve Young
8 Quarterback

Express had signed Steve Young. The whole limousine scene began to make sense.

"That's why he was in the mood he was in," says Seurer.

Ouch.

• • •

Bill Oldenburg may not have done many things right during his tenure as owner of the Los Angeles Express. But when it came to holding press conferences, this guy was a first-team all-American. When IMI moved into the California Street offices, Oldenburg hosted a press gathering complete with cocktails and caviar. Nelson Riddle's 34-piece band played and Wayne Newton sang "The Impossible Dream." To herald the signing of Steve Young on March 5, Oldenburg rented the Beverly Hilton's grand ballroom, provided a spread of food Orson Welles would have loved (he wasn't there, however). An open bar was another way of guaranteeing a large gathering, which there was. Young, wearing a tan jacket and brown tie—formal attire for him—came into the ballroom with TV cameras close behind. On the dais behind a battery of microphones, Young spoke briefly. Then Oldenburg and Klosterman took their turns, after which Young posed for pictures holding an Express uniform with his college number eight and his name sewn neatly on the back.

No contract terms were announced, but word had already leaked out. Forty-million was the number prevalently used to describe what the Express were paying Brigham Young's great-great-great grandson to play his football in the USFL. Mandel had taken a standard USFL contract, and then added pages of addendum for the particulars of this very unique deal. The beauty of all this is Young didn't exactly know how much money he was going to be paid. He knew it was a lot; he knew it was obscene. He didn't know it was $40 million, or $38 million, or $36.5 million, or whatever the contract amounted to. He'd never really even thought in terms of how much the contract was worth.

The media reported the breakdown of the $40 million contract, and soon the Express were confirming the reports. While Young was doing an interview with Los Angeles TV station KTLA, the interviewer talked about the $40 million contract. Young looked at the guy holding the mike, grabbed the handrail, and held on. He felt himself getting dizzy. It was the first time Young had heard the figure, and he was as overwhelmed as everybody else.

The contract:

- A signing bonus of $2.5 million ($1 million paid immediately upon signing of the contract and the remaining $1.5 million paid in three annual installments beginning in 1985);
- A no-interest loan of $1.5 million financed through State Savings and Loan in Utah (an S&L owned by Oldenburg) that would be repaid through Young's deferred money;
- A bonus of $275,000 for reporting to camp ($125,000 in 1984, $100,000 in 1985, and $50,000 in 1986);
- A base salary of $1.190 million over four years ($200,000 in 1984, $280,000 in 1985; $330,000 in 1986, and $380,000 in 1987);
- A scholarship fund totaling $183,000 established at Brigham Young University for a 20-year time period;

- Graduated annuities of $34.5 million paid over 37 years. The first payment of $200,000 would occur in 1990, with a final payment of $3.173 million by 2027).

All that together, bound into a tidy 15 pages signed by both Oldenburg and Young, made for a grand total of—drum roll, please—$40,145,000. That didn't even include the parking passes, the free tickets, and all the other minor details in the contract. Nor did it include the part of the contract that called for Young to donate $1,000 to local Los Angeles charities for each Express win, a sum the team agreed to match. If nothing else, Young was expected to reverse the Express' on-field performances.

"The Steve Young deal was different because of the amount of money and the time that it took, but it was really no different from a number of the other deals that we did," says Mandel.

At the top of the *New York Times* March 6, 1984 sports section, was a cartoon of a football center hiking bags of money to the quarterback. The caption said, "L.A. expresses its pleasure in Steve Young." Football was secondary at this point. The contract was the story. After all, this was still 1984. This was before Barry Bonds and Kirby Puckett and Glenn Robinson and Shaquille O'Neal. It sounded like the Express were talking about Monopoly money. *Forty-million.* If Young thought he had celebrity playing quarterback at BYU, it was nothing like the attention he'd receive as "The 40 Million Dollar Man."

In football circles, responses to the contract were mixed. John Bassett, founder of the defunct World Football League and owner of the USFL's Tampa Bay

Bandits, saw the Young signing as a repeat of his ill-fated attempt to gain credibility for the WFL when he coaxed Larry Csonka, Paul Warfield, and Jim Kiick to defect from the Miami Dolphins and the NFL to the WFL. It didn't work then, and Bassett wondered aloud why it would suddenly work a decade later.

Even USFL commissioner Chet Simmons, a Greenwich, Connecticut, resident, who had casually followed Young's high school and college careers, was worried about the amount of the contract. He told the Associated Press, "As commissioner, I don't like it. It worries me. I do not think it is in the best interest of professional football or the league, but what is to be done? These are wealthy businessmen seeking to build and sell a product and to compete." Others, like Washington Federals' owner Berl Bernhard, saw the Young signing as nothing more than a positive move and something of a stamp of approval for the league. That, too, was the way Young, Steinberg, and Oldenburg preferred to look at the contract.

Young was now wealthy enough that he could buy a home in Back Country Greenwich. He could buy a new car, update his wardrobe, forsake his passion for Burger King, and eat at the fashionable restaurants—all things he had no interest in doing. All Young wanted to do was play football.

A month after Young signed his contract, Jimmy Young, Steve's five-year-old brother, won an Easter egg-coloring contest he had entered in Greenwich. His prize was a crisp $5 bill. As Jimmy examined the contents of the envelope, he turned to his mom and said, "Wow, I'm as rich as Steve."

Not quite.

CHAPTER NINE

Eighty-Thousand Empty Seats

Steve Young didn't exactly strike an intimidating pose decked out in khaki pants, oxford shirt, and crew neck sweater while the rest of his Los Angeles Express teammates were suited up in football gear for their March 11 game with the Oakland Invaders. Young stood on the Oakland-Alameda Coliseum turf during pre-game warmups, less than a week after signing the richest contract in professional sports history, about as useful to the team as a fluorescent orange end zone pylon. The 40 Million Dollar Man watched quarterbacks Tom Ramsey and Frank Seurer throw the ball around the field before he retired to the sidelines to watch his new team, the Los Angeles Express, go three quarters without scoring a point. Just four months earlier, Young's BYU team would feel cheated if it went three minutes without putting points on the board. La-La land and the United States Football League, Young quickly realized, were going to be a lot different from Provo, Utah.

After signing the contract, Young had briefly considered not reporting to the club. He had been disenchanted with some of Oldenburg's displays, and was overwhelmed by the publicity, much of it negative, sur-rounding the signing. On the flight back to Utah, he broke down and cried. The accusations of greed leveled at Young by people who read and heard stories about "40 million dollars" and assumed Young was nothing more than a money grubber were especially painful. By virtue of the contract, Young was being held up as an example of what was wrong with American sports. More than anything, Young wanted to be the paradigm for what was right with them.

Says former Express offensive lineman Mark Adickes, who was a rookie alongside Young, "Steve was cursed with having to read the papers. He had to read them all the time. Everything written in those papers hurt him if it was negative. And I'm sure it really pleased him if it was positive."

Young did eventually report, at the urging of his fa-ther. "You signed a contract. You have to honor it," Grit Young said. That was all Young needed to hear.

Young was now a professional football player, play-ing for—watching, actually—the Los Angeles Express, who were being shut out. On the bright side Oakland couldn't score either. Express kicker Tony Zendejas broke the scoreless tie when he nailed a 40-yard field goal with 4:06 remaining in the fourth quarter, in a game the Express eventually won, 10-0. But Young felt empty. He remembered the ecstasy of his final game at Cougar Stadium when 65,000 fans cheered as he bid farewell to the BYU faithful. Then there was the feeling he had as he ran around like a little kid after catching the winning pass against Missouri in the Holiday Bowl a month later. Now he was standing in street clothes in this huge sta-dium in Oakland, California, realizing that 9,000 people in such a cavernous place don't make much noise. In fact, they gave the place kind of an eerie feeling. Even in the upbeat Express locker room after the win, Young didn't fit in. He didn't know many of his teammates yet, so he sat there with an unemotional smile on his face, feeling nothing.

Frank Seurer felt something. His performance wasn't a thing of beauty, but in his first professional start, the rookie quarterback finished the game having completed 21 of 37 passes for 185 yards. Not bad. His problem was interceptions; he completed three to Oakland defenders. There would be no visit to Bill Oldenburg's limo after this game. Los Angeles also fumbled five times, losing three, in a game generously termed ugly. In spite of the win, and his performance, it was clear to Seurer that he was merely keeping the seat warm until Young was ready to take over. When that would happen was the big question.

John Hadl, who had coached Seurer at the University of Kansas, had confidence in his rookie quarterback and felt comfortable with Seurer running the show. Hadl also realized you don't give Young the kind of money the Express were paying and then sit him on the bench. Seurer was indeed a lame duck, and Hadl knew it. In discussions with Sid Gillman and Don Klosterman, Hadl decided to bring Young along slowly. Although he had been playing at BYU into December and had kept himself in playing shape, his late signing precluded attending training camp with the rest of the Express players. The consensus opinion of the Express braintrust was that they didn't want to play Young until he was more comfortable with Los Angeles' one-back offense. The truth was, the signing of Young had caused a lot of publicity for a team badly in need of that sort of thing, and it would have been nice to ride the Steve Young wave of momentum by playing him immediately. The Express were not drawing well at home, and there really weren't any other big-name players fans would pay to see. Still, with a long-term gameplan in place, Hadl chose to sit Young and sequester him in the film room with Gillman. If Young thought he could recognize coverages while playing quarterback at BYU, Gillman had news for him. The Father of the Modern Passing Game had a new son. Young would study what Gillman was telling him, and then try to execute it in practice. Young would have to be patient.

The "bring Young along slowly" plan was difficult to stick to the following week against the San Antonio Gunslingers in Alamo Stadium. Seurer struggled through the first half, and Tom Ramsey relieved him midway through the third period. Ironically, it was Seurer who replaced Ramsey two weeks earlier against Birmingham at almost the same juncture of that game. When Ramsey entered this game, he got the offense rolling. The former UCLA quarterback engineered two fourth-quarter drives that resulted in field goals, the last coming with only 1:09 left to give the Express a come-from-behind 13-12 win. The Express' quarterback problem was far from solved. For his part, Young did his best to support the team by patting players on the helmets and cheering when the Express scored. That was all he could do. Watching the game from the sidelines in street clothes prevented him from doing anything else. After waiting his turn at BYU, and now doing the same with Los Angeles, Young decided standing and watching was no way to play football.

With the win against San Antonio secured, Hadl indicated Seurer would be the Express' starting quarterback in the following week's game in the Coliseum against Jacksonville. Hadl's pronouncement was loud and clear; Young would not play. He did hint, however, that Young would see his first USFL game action the following week when the New Jersey Generals came to town for an April Fools' Day contest in the Coliseum. True to his word, Hadl went with Seurer as his starter against the Bulls. And without Young as a drawing card, the Express' marketing department promoted a postgame concert featuring Chuck Berry, the Coasters, and Freddy (Boom Boom) Cannon, an event they hoped would go better than the concert the Express staged after the season-opener. Wayne Newton had performed *Danke Schoen* and some of his other classics to about 80,000 empty Coliseum seats following a 27-10 loss to the Denver Gold.

Against Birmingham, 16,042 people passed through the turnstiles to watch the Express' anemic offense score one touchdown in a 13-7 loss to the Bulls. Incredibly, Chuck, Boom Boom, and the Coasters put on a better show than the Express. Something needed to be done. The offense was struggling to get the ball in the end zone, and the team's small fan following was getting restless. With that in mind Steve Young was handed the reins. The 40 Million Dollar Man was dispatching the Seurer-Ramsey platoon to the bench.

"Obviously when you sign somebody like Steve Young for the amount of money that they paid for him, he's going to play," says Seurer. "I'm not sure Steve wouldn't have beaten me out anyway, because obviously he's a great quarterback.

"But I knew inside that I really didn't have a chance to compete for the job after that. That's the way it worked."

The team needed a shot in the arm, and so did the franchise. With New Jersey coming to town, and with Young named the starter, there was actually a little bit of excitement surrounding the game pitting New Jersey vs. Los Angeles, Steve Young vs. Herschel Walker, quarterback vs. running back. Walker had been the league's 1983 version of Steve Young, a high-profile player jumping from college to the USFL. To have Young and Walker on the field at the same time made sense, mostly because of the marketing possibilities. Young vs. Walker would create natural interest for a league losing credibility in the minds of America's sports fans. Adding additional intrigue was the fact that the league's two most highly visible and outspoken owners were the Generals' Donald Trump and the Express' Oldenburg. The Express also did something unique to promote the game. They offered a two-tickets-for-the-price-of-one deal on all $8 and $11 seats, and took out ads in newspapers and on television telling fans to "Catch Steve Young's First Pass."

An ordinary fan probably could have caught one of Young's passes against the Generals. He completed 19 of 29 passes, mainly from the shotgun formation, for 163 yards, with one touchdown, and one interception in a 26-10 loss. He even completed seven consecutive passes in one second-quarter stretch, resulting in the team's lone touchdown. However, Hadl and Gillman, running a very conservative offensive package, didn't allow their star QB to throw a pass longer than 10 yards the entire game. Young led the team in rushing, picking up 32 yards on 16 carries. Despite all that, Los Angeles only scored 10 points. The loss ended their modest two-game winning streak, and they also lost at the gate. The two-for-one scheme hadn't worked very well, with only 19,583 showing up. Even with all that, it had felt good for Young to get on the field and play. The histrionics were finally starting to die down, and people were beginning to focus on football instead of money.

The thought of whether he had made the right decision joining the Express continually gnawed at Young. Should he have waited for the NFL draft? Was he too hasty in his decision? These were unanswerable questions at this late date. The NFL beckoned for Young in June when he was the first pick in the NFL's supplemental draft of USFL and Canadian Football League players. The Tampa Bay Buccaneers had the first pick, and Buccaneer Coach John McKay, having liked Young when he played at BYU, and having seen him play a couple of USFL games, selected Young. Young would be one of 11 Express players selected in the first 25 picks. All told, 20 of the 84 players chosen in the special draft were Express players, with Young being the creme de la creme. On June 4 agent Leigh Steinberg notified Young that Tampa Bay owned his NFL rights, news that immediately intrigued both men. Young thought back to McKay's glory days as coach of the USC Trojans, and he was flattered by the things Steinberg said McKay had said about him. The NFL dream for Young was still there, and now the NFL felt that much closer. It was also a long way away. The NFL would just have to wait.

After a three-week getting-to-know-you period, Young began to fit in with the team. After signing with the Express, Young moved into a hotel near the Los Angeles International Airport before renting an apartment in a Manhattan Beach complex called Harbor Cove. Also living in apartments there were offensive linemen Adickes, Mike Ruether, Gary Zimmerman, and tight end Gordon Hudson. All four, like Young, had been first-round supplemental selections by the NFL. Hudson was selected by Seattle, Zimmerman went two picks after Young to the New York Giants, Adickes was the fifth pick to Kansas City, and Ruether was chosen by St. Louis as the number-17 choice. To say some talent was living in Harbor Cove would be grossly understating the situation. They were also good guys, and Young found a comfort zone. But something didn't feel totally right, and his teammates recognized it. Young felt like he had been strongarmed into signing the contract, and he knew he didn't like Oldenburg at all. For everybody who thinks money will buy happiness, Young was a poster child against that belief. To quote Young's great-great-great grandfather, "The possession of wealth alone does not produce happiness . . . although it will produce comfort." Indeed. Young, a 22-year-old millionaire, was happier when he was at BYU, eating cookies, playing video games, watching "Hawaii Five-0" reruns, and scrounging money so he could buy pizza.

Almost immediately after signing their contracts, Zimmerman and Adickes bought Porsche 911s. Adickes' was white, Zimmerman's, red. Meanwhile, Young was trying to arrange to get his Oldsmobile out to California.

"It took us all two years to talk him into buying a new car. And he would not get rid of the Oldsmobile and get something new for anything," says Seurer.

"We all bought waterbeds, stereos, and TVs. Young didn't partake in any of this. He bought nothing. He rented a place that already had a TV, a stereo, and a bed," says Adickes. "Oddly enough, the guy signs for $40 million, we would go out to eat and he'd never have money. He used to rent movies and then forget to bring them back. So he'd rent a movie for one night, and it would end up costing him a hundred bucks because he'd keep forgetting to bring it back."

"He had more money than God, but he wasn't flamboyant by any means," Seurer adds.

In other words, Young was no Bill Oldenburg. Then again, who was? After watching his team's record drop to 2-4 for the season, Oldenburg started getting fidgety. In fact, he was squirming. The owner wasn't happy with his club's on-field performance, and he expected a better showing when he traveled with the Express to Denver for a Monday night game against the Gold in Mile High Stadium on April 9. He decided the "Best Young Team in Football" better do something, quickly. The Gold came into the game with a 5-1 record, and had every intention of improving to 6-1 against the youngsters from Los Angeles.

With the Express, you weren't sure what you were going to get—a residual effect of talent mixed with inexperience. Says Adickes, "The problem was you had no nucleus. You had all these college kids who had come together and didn't know what was expected of them. An immature team doesn't respond well. John Hadl was a great guy and a player's coach. But young players are too immature to perform for a coach who is so good to them." That would explain why Los Angeles would look like world beaters one minute, and then pull a Three Stooges act the next.

This game followed form. The Express opened the game looking like championship contenders, much to the delight of Oldenburg who watched from his private box, and the dismay of 19,115 Denver fans sitting in the pouring rain. They were not only showing an offensive pulse, they were breathing without a respirator. The Express had only scored 54 points in their first five games, and here they scored two touchdowns in the game's first 11 minutes. The offense was clicking with Young calling the shots, and the Express defense was neutralizing the Gold. Oldenburg was positively giddy.

Then just as quickly, things turned sour. Trailing 14-7, the Gold scored 18 unanswered points in the final 3:39 of the first half as nobody from Los Angeles could hang onto the ball. What had started so promising ended with the Express trailing 25-14 at the half. The Express had delivered the kind of spotty first-half play fans had come to expect from such a young team. The inexperience issue didn't seem to matter to Oldenburg, though. His team had been ahead, it was now behind, and he wanted to know why. Basically, he had the Express on a very short leash.

In the locker room, coach Hadl told his players not to get down and to go out in the second half and do what they had done in the first quarter. It was a normal halftime speech. Normal, that is, until Oldenburg showed up. Already full of too much alcohol, Oldenburg took the floor and delivered a speech that wasn't exactly "Win one for the Gipper." More to the point, Oldenburg's tirade reminded Young a lot of his dealings with the Express owner during his contract negotiations.

"Now dammit, John, wait a minute," Oldenburg began. "Let me talk to these sons of bitches." It got worse from there. Oldenburg castigated the entire team, and told everybody they wouldn't be around after the game if they didn't play better in the second half. Hadl stood in disbelief as his boss, who really knew nothing about football, ranted and raved at the Express players. Three minutes later, Oldenburg was done. No sooner had the owner arrived than he was gone. Trying to maintain some dignity in the middle of a bad situation, Hadl rubbed his eyes and said, "Well boys, don't let that guy get to you." Nobody did.

"We all just looked at each other and shook our heads. You could look in John Hadl's face and see how irritated he was at the whole thing. You could tell how bad he wanted to just say something and get Oldenburg out of there," says Seurer. "We were just amazed at how someone like him could run an organization like this. It just didn't make sense. I don't know of anybody who really got along with Bill Oldenburg and respected how he was."

After (or despite) Oldenburg's tantrum, the Express offense came out in the second half and tacked on two more scores, including a beautiful 69-yard scoring strike from Young to Kevin Nelson with 13:59 remaining in the third quarter. But they could never come all the way back, and finally lost the game, 35-27. Young, who rushed for 34 yards, was sacked three times, and had to suffer through the embarrassment of throwing a pass that slipped out of his hands and squirted high into the air. Much to his chagrin, that play was shown on every news highlight reel that evening. Young ended up completing just 16 of 37 passes for 267 yards. But maybe the loss was a blessing. For whatever reason, the Express turned things around beginning the following week. Oldenburg was sadly mistaken if he thought his impromptu halftime speech had inspired his players.

What may have prompted Oldenburg's outburst was the pecuniary squeeze he was beginning to feel. Rumblings around the league about Oldenburg's financial situations were not flattering. The picture Oldenburg had painted when he bought the Express was much different from the way things really were.

IMI wasn't the cash cow Oldenburg told everybody it was, and in reality the company had recently been on a three-year money losing streak. Some creative financial statements had earned Oldenburg entrance into the USFL's owners' club, and at the time there seemed no reason to question Oldenburg's alleged wealth. In the Express' game programs, Oldenburg's short biography called him a "self-made billionaire." The title above that same bio read, "Meet Mr. Dynamite," whatever that meant. It was interesting reading, if you liked fiction.

The rumors of money problems were eventually justified. The 46-year-old professional football team owner may have driven a Rolls Royce to work, and he may have signed Steve Young to the most lucrative contract in the history of professional sports, but J. William Oldenburg was no billionaire. Nobody at IMI was banging the gong.

The Express players tried to forget all the peripheral problems, and chose to deal instead with things on the field. It worked for one week as Los Angeles got a 22-for-34 passing performance from Young that resulted in 358 passing yards and a 23-17 overtime win over the Memphis Showboats. Young scored the winning touchdown and connected on an 81-yard touchdown hookup with Jojo Townsell, for the longest completion in the USFL that year. Young also rushed for 24 yards, giving him 382 total offense yards, a new Express single-game record. The following week, though, it was more bad publicity for the Express, and this time Young was right in the middle of it.

In a telephone conference call with Chicago-area reporters who were working on stories for the Express-Chicago Blitz game on April 20, Young said, "I really feel like the NFL is going to quietly take on about four or five teams—very exciting ballclubs—and then watch the rest of the league sort of fall by the wayside." That statement got the reporters' attention, and they were a rapt audience by the time Young finished. "I still have that dream and my dream now is to take this team into the NFL. That will be my next challenge." Young added a few more tidbits, without trying to backpedal.

It was the worst possible news for a beleaguered league and franchise, giving more fodder to a bunch of reporters from a city with the USFL's weakest franchise. The Chicago Blitz were averaging a little less than 8,000 fans in 65,000-seat Soldier Field, and they looked like a prime candidate to sort of "fall by the wayside." The following day, after a spate of stories in newspapers and on radio and television detailing Young's comments, a repentant Young began his retraction. But by then the damage had been done. "I got involved in league politics and I shouldn't have," Young told the Associated Press. "I learned my lesson, and I'll bear the brunt for it. I'm not perfect. But you've got to be careful what you say. I will from now on." The next evening, following Young's arrival in Chicago with the rest of the team, the Express scheduled a hastily arranged press conference where Young continued his mea culpa routine. "I guess I threw an interception there, but we'll just have to recover." Young continued by expressing how happy he was playing for the Express, and that he had no regrets signing with the upstart league. Young had done what he had to do to make the best of a bad situation, yet Herb Vincent, the Express' assistant media relations director, knew how Young really felt.

"Steve would come in our office a lot and he'd spend a lot of time talking to Express media relations director Bob Rose. Steve would come in every day wanting to know what was going on with the league, what was the latest word from New York, what was going on with the TV contract. He was real, real concerned with the business end of it," says Vincent. "But it was stuff he should have been concerned about because he was one of the league's marquee players and he was *the* marquee player with the Express."

Whatever faux pas Young had committed by speaking his mind, didn't affect his play against the Blitz. In only his fourth professional start, Young threw for 302 yards and one touchdown on 25-of-37 passing. He also broke Kevin Nelson's Express team rushing record by running for 120 yards on 16 carries. Young became the first professional football player in history to pass for 300 yards and rush for 100 in the same game. Despite Young's heroics, the Express were 49-29 losers. No matter what they did, it seemed the Express couldn't catch a break.

Two weeks later, the scrutiny of Oldenburg really began. Coming into question was a real estate transaction involving the sale of 363 acres of undeveloped property in Richmond, California, made by Oldenburg's Investment Mortgage International to State Savings & Loan, the same S&L owned by Oldenburg that gave Young the interest-free loan stipulated in his $40 million contract. IMI had sold the property for $55 million to State Savings, after initially purchasing the land for $800,000 in 1977. The Utah Department of Financial Institutions concluded State Savings broke a state regulation when it purchased land that cost more than ten percent of its assets. Also a bit fishy was one Oldenburg entity selling property to another Oldenburg entity for a neat little profit. Investigations resulted, and within a month Oldenburg stepped down as a director and chairman of the board of State Savings & Loan. Less than a week after that, State Savings & Loan was put up for sale.

• • •

The Los Angeles Express were 3-6 and going nowhere fast. The inexperience of the team, instead of the talent, was having its way, and was evident on the field and off. The Express desperately needed something good to occur, and it did in the form of an eight-game stretch where the Express won seven times, captured the Pacific Division title, and clinched a playoff berth. Winning was a panacea for Express players. Finally the game became fun, especially for Young. As the wins kept piling up, the quarterbacks, Young and Seurer, would occasionally buy dinner for the offensive line. They'd also pop for the drinks. At those dinners it became customary for veteran tackle Jeff Hart to speak for a few minutes before the meal.

"Let's go out and kick some butt this week," Hart would say. He'd then propose a toast and insist each player take a shot—usually of tequila. Later in the week, they'd go out and kick some butt. Young would always participate in the toasts, substituting 7-Up or Sprite for the liquor. Offensive lineman Derek Kennard would notice how much soda pop Young could throw down.

"That's just how he was," Seurer says. "He was a strong, religious person. We totally respected his religious beliefs."

That respect didn't stop Express players from trying to get Young to enjoy a little of the Los Angeles night scene on occasion. One of the first things Mark Adickes, Mike Ruether, Hart, and Seurer noticed about Young was how simply he lived. He didn't go out much, and seemed to focus entirely on football. That, they decided, had to change.

"There was many a time where we tried to set Steve up with different girls because he didn't date much. He just didn't like talking to girls. But whenever we did get a chance to take him with us to a night club, we'd always have fun with him. He was so naive and he couldn't believe how the girls would dress. We'd try to get him out there dancing and he'd say, 'No, no. I'm not going to do that.' It was a whole different world for him, and it was just fun having him around for that. A lot of times we thought the whole thing was an act, but then we realized, man, that's just how he is."

The winning streak had relaxed the entire team. Maybe what made things so loose in the Express camp was the absence of Oldenburg, who hadn't attended his team's games since his drunken halftime tongue-lashing in Denver. Amid wild speculation about his and the team's financial stability, Oldenburg had purposely kept a low profile. That changed at the Express' home game in the Coliseum against the Oakland Invaders. Oldenburg refused to speak to reporters before the game, and afterward, he made his way to the locker room to congratulate the team on its latest triumph, a 24-19 win. He primarily sought out Young to compliment him on his performance where he completed 14 of 16 passes (87 percent) for 194 yards, while carrying the ball eight times for 82 yards.

Young had seen enough of Oldenburg's previous performances to know he wanted no part of the owner. So Young bunkered himself in the shower, and even conducted post-game interviews in his tiled sanctum safely away from Bill Oldenburg. Young soon learned he could run but he couldn't hide, and after a short game of dodge ball the star quarterback and the owner met. In his excitement Oldenburg tried to give Young a hug, but Young struck the Heisman pose and straight-armed the owner in the chest. Oldenburg took the hint, and extended his hand. Young, reluctantly, shook it. For a locker room with hot showers running, things still felt pretty icy.

In the playoffs, the Express drew the defending USFL champion Michigan Panthers as their first-round opponent. The two would go at it on June 30 in the Los Angeles Coliseum. It was a game for the ages, lasting four hours, four minutes in real time, 93:33 in football time. The Express defeated the Panthers, 27-21, when Mel Gray scored on a scintillating 24-yard touchdown run in the third overtime after Michigan kicker Novo Bojovic missed two medium-range field goals in overtime. The Express players were overcome with the emotion of playing in the longest game in professional football history. Some even may have suffered from delirium—Young included. Amid the celebrating in the locker room, Bill Oldenburg found Young and the two men dispensed with the handshakes and embraced. It was that kind of day. Oldenburg finally got his hug, he just had to wait a week for it. Young finished 23 of 44 for 295 yards in the passing department, and rushed for 44 yards. The win earned the Express the right to play the Arizona Wranglers for the Western Conference championship. It was a game the Express were supposed to host. Instead, they packed their bags for the road.

The day the conference championship game was to be played, the Los Angeles Coliseum had been reserved for Summer Olympics preparation, and the Rose Bowl in nearby Pasadena was undergoing turf sodding. Meanwhile, the Los Angeles Rams, who had already reserved Anaheim Stadium for a season-ticket function of their own, wouldn't rearrange their schedule for their USFL rival. Out of options, the Express were exiled to Tempe, Arizona, for a home playoff game in Sun Devil Stadium on the campus of Arizona State University on July 7. Not only would they be playing for the conference championship away from home, they'd be doing it in the scorching desert heat. The only solace came when the league changed kickoff from 12:30 P.M. to 8:30 that night for health considerations. Instead of playing football in 120-degree weather, the Express and the Wranglers would get it on in pleasant, balmy 100-degree conditions. This game would not conjure up any images of a snow-covered Lambeau Field in Green Bay, Wisconsin. That much was certain.

The heat was the last thing worrying Young. He'd endured the brutal heat of Las Vegas in BYU's 1982 season-opener during his junior year, as well as the hellish humidity of Athens, Georgia, for the Cougars' game between the hedges against Georgia. No, the heat wasn't an issue in Young's mind. Neither was the fear the

Express wouldn't be able to score against Arizona. The question most concering Young was, Could the Los Angeles defense stop the Wranglers' offense?

For a while it looked like the Express defense would hold up. They held a 17-7 lead despite a shaky game from Young, who finished completing only 7 of 23 passes for 123 yards. However, as the game wore on, the Wranglers proved too much, scoring 21 unanswered points to go ahead 28-17 in what would eventually end as a 35-23 win for the George Allen-coached Wranglers. In the days leading up to the game, much of the focus was on whether Allen had actually put out a bounty on Young, offering financial incentives to any player who could knock Young from the game. Allen denied everything, but he didn't mind talking about it. It was the sort of gamesmanship he thought might rattle the rookie quarterback and give Arizona an advantage.

In the loss, Young came away unscathed, with none of the hits by Arizona defenders looking out of the ordinary. Whether Young was intimidated by all the pre-game bounty talk wasn't readily apparent. But Allen knew his front seven had sacked Young seven times, had allowed completions on only 30 percent of his passes, and his Wranglers, not the Express, would be playing for the league title.

While Arizona moved on, the Express cleaned out their lockers. The season was finally history, and it had been a wild year for the Pacific Division champs. While NFL teams were getting ready for the preseason, the Express players were going their separate ways. Football Los Angeles Express style would be put on hold for six months. The Oldenburg cloud hanging over the team was as gray as ever, yet the franchise would live to see another season, even if the people of Los Angeles had proven during the first two years they had no interest in supporting a USFL franchise, even an exciting one.

For Steve Young, his first year as a professional had been anything but boring. He was still better known for his contract with all the zeroes than he was for guiding the Express to the playoffs. But, Young had clearly made a difference once he became acclimated to the team and its offense. Nobody was yet saying Young was worth all the money he was being paid. But nobody was saying he wasn't either.

CHAPTER TEN

Can't Buy Me Happiness

Steve Young's professional football odyssey began in February of 1984 and ended at least temporarily on a sweltering day in Tempe, Arizona. That first USFL season had gone by so fast, and so many things had happened. There was the money, the new team, Bill Oldenburg. Young couldn't wait to get out of Los Angeles and back to somewhere familiar. Provo, Utah, seemed right to him. He was still a few hours short of graduating, and wanted to finish. He had also signed on with KBYU, the BYU-based Public Broadcasting System station, to provide color commentary for BYU football games.

Young had often told people after his eligibility at BYU had expired that he would have been happy playing college football forever and not doing anything else. He was dead serious. After everything he'd been through in that initial season with the Express, Young gladly would have gone back to BYU to play. Of course, after that initial season with the Express Young probably would have been happy in Tibet playing football with a ball made from the bladder of a yak as long as Bill Oldenburg wasn't around.

In Provo, Young was free from the Express, at least temporarily. While he was there, he sat in a press box booth alongside play-by-play man Jay Monsen and called for Channel 11 viewers the most miraculous of all BYU football seasons.

Young broadcast all six home games that season, traveled with the team to Hawaii for the game with the Rainbows, and also worked the Holiday Bowl that sealed the national championship for the Cougars when they beat Michigan. Young was bright and articulate in the booth, and provided a lot of anecdotal information for viewers that only a former player could. Young spent time in team meetings and visited with former teammates so he'd have interesting things to say. He could have taken the easy way by simply showing up, saying a few things each game, and staying out of Monsen's way. Instead, like everything else in Young's life, he was prepared. He did his homework, and he came across well. He wasn't a blatant homer, but he did want the Cougars to win. During the course of the season, Monsen noticed how agitated Young would get when the Cougars would turn the ball over, and how excited he'd get when they'd score.

In the Holiday Bowl, BYU quarterback Robbie Bosco, who had apprenticed under Young the previous year, was injured early in the game against the Wolverines only to come back and lead the Cougars to a last-minute victory, ensuring the Cougars a perfect 13-0 season. At the conclusion of games, KBYU generally ran public service announcements or trailers for upcoming shows and then would return for a short, 90-second wrapup of the game. That night, Monsen was forced to do the wrapup alone. No sooner had

BYU players rushed onto the field for a post-game celebration than Young bolted from the press box to join
in on the festivities. That entire 1984 BYU season made
Young homesick. The Cougars were having the kind of
fun he used to have, and now he wasn't a part of it.
Even worse, he knew that soon he'd have to report
back to Manhattan Beach to prepare for the 1985 USFL
season.

It had been a good offseason. His alma mater won
the national title, and Young earned his degree. He graduated with a Bachelor of Arts in international relations on
December 15, right before he left for the Holiday Bowl.

With snow on the ground in Provo and Christmas
lights everywhere, preseason football, along with roasting
chestnuts, was in the air, if by chance the USFL was your
game, which, sadly, it was for Young. Vacation was over
and it was back to work. Young decided to go to camp
optimistic that things would improve over the previous
season. It was a good idea, but his put-on-a-happy-face
outlook didn't last long.

If Steve Young and the other Los Angeles Express
players were hoping their 1985 United States Football
League experience would be less volatile than the previous one, they were in for a big disappointment. The
1985 version of the Los Angeles Express would be to stability what Orson Welles was to dieting. Things for the
Express began deteriorating 17 days after the loss to
Arizona ended their 1984 season. Defensive coordinator
Ray Malavasi was fired, mainly because of financial
problems within the franchise. Preceding Malavasi's
ouster, 13 Express front-office employees, mostly marketing types, had also been given their pink slips. People
making $25,000 or $30,000 a year were being let go to

ease the team's financial burden while Steve Young was waiting for a $1.5 million annuity payment from the team, due on September 15. It was the proverbial case of someone stepping over a dollar bill to pick up a dime.

Who would cover Young's annuity payment, as well as his salary, was another question. On July 22, 1984, the door had finally slammed shut on J. William Oldenburg when the league announced that Oldenburg, the self-proclaimed billionaire, had withdrawn as owner of the Los Angeles Express. "Mr. Dynamite" was a dud. With Oldenburg out of the picture, the league was left to assume de facto ownership of the team while it searched for potential buyers. Buyers weren't exactly lining up outside Commissioner Chet Simmons' office with check-books in hand. Who would want to buy into a moribund franchise with a bloated payroll? Who would want any-thing to do with a team that nobody in Los Angeles seemed to care about? With no new money on the hori-zon, the Los Angeles Express became the league's team. The other USFL owners had to chip in approximately $500,000 each from their own pockets to keep the fran-chise afloat, not out of a sense of devotion to the Express players or to the city but because the contract the USFL signed with ABC Television stipulated that a franchise be located in the Los Angeles market. The TV money was critical to the league's existence. In essence, the Express had been tossed a life preserver.

The clues that 1985 would be the Express' last season were everywhere. The attendance never got better for Los Angeles home games, and, in fact, be-came even more abysmal than the previous two years. On April 7, the Express hosted the defending league champion Baltimore Stars in the Coliseum and only

5,637 saw the Stars defeat the Express, 17-6. It was an all-time low attendance mark for the franchise. The week before that game, Herb Vincent, who had been promoted to media relations director when Bob Rose went to work for the league office, was driving to the Coliseum for the game against the Oakland Invaders. As Vincent pulled into the Coliseum parking lot two hours before kickoff, he noticed a lot full of cars, scalpers hawking tickets, and people standing in line outside the stadium. Vincent was mystified. Scalpers at an Express game? he thought. Vincent drove a bit farther when he suddenly realized the people standing in line weren't going to the Coliseum after all. Instead, they were facing the L.A. Sports Arena next door—taking their interest and their wallets with them to the World Wrestling Federation's Wrestlemania, being broadcast on closed-circuit television from New York. Apparently 8,500 people wanted to spend their Sunday inside watching Hulk Hogan and Mr. T put the hurt on Rowdy Roddy Piper and Paul "Mr. Wonderful" Orndorff. Across the way, the Express lost to Oakland before 11,619, an attendance figure about as legitimate as a Shanghai Sleeper hold.

A few weeks later, while the Express practiced at their Manhattan Beach training facility, Young watched three moving vans pull up in front of the team's offices. Within minutes, the movers came out with furniture and equipment. Young noticed his teammates, who had quit practicing to observe the proceedings. They all had the same look on their faces.

"We were all just unbelievably amazed. We just looked at each other and kind of chuckled. But at the same time we were scared. We were like, 'Okay, what exactly is going on here?'" says Frank Seurer, the backup quarterback.

Actually, the players knew exactly what was going on. All the Express players got their paychecks on a regular basis every Monday, but they'd heard enough about creditors lining up for payment to know the Express' financial picture was less than perfect. Quick deduction told them a furniture rental company had not been paid by the team. Strangely, as the movers did their work, a case of champagne was delivered to the players from a devoted Express fan who knew nothing of what was going on with the repo men. Included along with the champagne was a note. "Guys, keep up the good work. We're still behind you," it said. Right then, coach John Hadl decided the team had practiced long enough. He opened the box and began distributing bottles. Hadl said, "Here's to you. You can't win 'em all." The players popped the corks and had an impromptu party. Young participated with a cup of water.

By then, Young knew even if the United States Football League survived, the Los Angeles Express were history. The writing was on the wall, only the Express couldn't afford the pencils.

• • •

During his one-plus years with the Express, Young remained a positive influence on the team. He tried to be as upbeat as possible despite the impossible situation. But, he also studied his options. Tampa Bay was a possibility. His interest had been piqued when the Bucs selected him the year before, and nothing had changed since. Yet he still had a job to do with the Express, no matter how dire things became.

"Steve was fabulous. He was tremendous and so down-to-earth. That's what struck me about him all the time. He had no ego whatsoever. He was always unassuming, and he didn't look like a rich millionaire or anything. He was just one of the guys," says Vincent, who dealt with Young on an almost daily basis.

"Steve was our real leader. He was the guy that everybody looked up to and everybody respected. He could do it all. He could run, he could throw, he was smart, and he was tough," says Seurer. "I was almost jealous of him because I wasn't looked at the same way he was. As a quarterback, you want to be a leader. I got respect when I played, but the Express players looked at Steve as our real leader."

Eventually, the losing began to take its toll on Young. For a team that had gone to the conference championship game the year before with players any NFL general manager would want, the 1985 Los Angeles Express season was a brutal awakening to how quickly things can go into the toilet. Los Angeles opened the season with three straight losses before finally breaking into the win column against the San Antonio Gunslingers in a game the *Boston Globe* reported would be the team's denouement. It wasn't. Young fully expected that first win to be a jump-off point for a winning streak similar to the one they had pulled off the previous year. Young's theory was flawed, though. He hadn't factored injuries—especially his own—into that equation.

In Tempe for a game with Arizona, now nicknamed the Outlaws, on March 23, Young went down in a heap near the left sideline with 3:59 remaining in the third quarter. He'd just made an 18-yard-run when disaster struck. The former Greenwich High wishbone quarterback never did learn the quarterback hook slide that could have helped him avoid a few dangerous collisions. At Greenwich High, Young learned that taking a hit came with the position. At BYU, coach LaVell Edwards occasionally suggested Young go down instead of taking on every would-be tackler for the sake of a few extra yards. Ted Tollner and Mike Holmgren, Young's quarterback coaches at BYU, would second that advice. In the pros, Hadl gave his quarterback the same lecture. Yet Young felt he was invincible. He also reasoned that he could juke anybody with a bead on him anyway, and avoid a direct shot. It had worked when he was an eight-year-old playing on Lone Peak Drive. He wasn't about to change his philosophy now that he was getting paid to play football. Young's views on running the ball even worked for a while. His injuries were just the obligatory bumps and bruises that came with the position until Arizona cornerback Carl Allen nailed Young hard and left the quarterback with a pain in his knee he'd never felt before.

What else could go wrong? Hadl thought, as he looked at his star player crumpled on the Sun Devil Stadium turf, writhing in pain. The damage—strained ligaments to Young's left knee. The injury wouldn't require surgery; it would, however, knock Young from the game. He watched into the fourth quarter on crutches with a splint on his knee before finally hobbling into the locker room when it became too painful. It wasn't his knee causing the pain. The Express were losing and Young was helpless to do anything about it. The situation felt a lot like when he had first arrived in Los Angeles after signing the big contract. All he could do was stand and watch.

"I remember Steve making the remark to me, 'I've never been hurt before.' He couldn't fathom being hurt. He couldn't understand why a quarterback wasn't supposed to run the ball. I think he learned from the injury. I think it was a shock to him the first time he did get hurt because he had never been in that situation before," says Vincent.

After team orthopedist, Dr. James Tibone, issued a post-game, week-by-week evaluation of the injury, Young came back with his own prognosis. In the locker room following the 27-13 loss to Arizona, Young told reporters he thought he'd play the following week. He was wrong, by three weeks. This wasn't like his shoulder injury in high school. This one would take some time to heal.

Young's injury earned him select membership into a growing club of Express players who were spending a majority of their time in the trainer's room. Injuries had come in bunches all season, and the team's superstar apparently wasn't immune. All Young could do was join the other "knees" on the sideline. Offensive linemen Jeff Hart and Derek Kennard, defensive lineman Joe Lukens, wide receivers Duane Gunn and LeRoy Campbell, and linebacker Kevin Turner all had bad wheels. A litany of other players were also banged up, with injuries covering practically the entire human anatomy. Running back Robert Alexander (hamstring), cornerback Wymon Henderson (groin), defensive end Ray Cattage (elbow), and H-back Tony Boddie (foot) kept the trainers busy. Even more insulting than the injuries was the league's refusal to allow Express general manager Don Klosterman to sign new players to replace the injured. If desks and filing cabinets were being hauled out of the Express' headquarters with the league's blessing, it was clear the USFL wasn't about to let Klosterman go shopping for new players with the other owners' hard-earned money. The signing moratorium meant no new quarterbacks. When Young went down with his knee problem, backup Frank Seurer, the only other QB on the roster, was forced into action. Presumably coach John Hadl, the former all-pro quarterback, was his backup.

Young did eventually return to the lineup, and his performance in his first game back was dubious at best. Attrition had left the Express as one of the league's worst teams; the "best young team in football" moniker no longer fit. Against the Denver Gold, Young made the start and reinjured the same knee early in the second quarter after completing 5 of 10 passes for 69 yards. He was also sacked six times before, in a humane gesture, being removed from the game. The Express were waxed, 51-0.

Young played the following week against the Portland Breakers in a game that was widely speculated as Los Angeles' final hurrah. Even Hadl had told the players in the locker room before the game as much. The Express would win that game, the franchise's last victory ever. But it wasn't their last game. In a surprise move, the league elected to continue subsidizing the team through the end of the year. To Young, it didn't matter. By then, the end was near. He was certain of it.

Before their next game against the Tampa Bay Bandits, Young and Seurer soft-tossed the ball back and forth inside the Coliseum. Suddenly, Young stopped and began laughing. Surveying the thousands and thousands of empty seats, Young spotted two of his buddies sitting in the stands. Not long afterward, Seurer, a southern

California native, found his brother and several other friends in the far-from-madding crowd. It became a game between the two to see who could spot the most people. Find-A-Friend was a contest Seurer would win. In the spacious stadium, the two quarterbacks shook their heads and laughed at the absurdity of the situation. They were standing in a 92,000-seat stadium easily picking out familiar faces in the announced crowd of 4,912. The Bandits beat up on the Express, 24-14. Never did a game feel less like pro football.

"It was so demoralizing to see what was happening around us. We knew it wasn't going to last long, that this was going to be it. Maybe it should have made it easier to focus on just playing, relaxing, and not worrying about things," recalls Seurer. "I really think we had a hard time focusing on what we were doing. I think it just wore on everybody. We all dragged around a lot. Practices were really sluggish. We just didn't have the heart and the energy anymore. It just wasn't there."

"Everyone knew our situation was really tenuous, that our paychecks could bounce and the team could fold. So I think it just sapped whatever spirit and emotion the players had. I think that's probably why there were so many injuries, and one of the big reasons why the team did so poorly," says Adickes. "I don't think anybody put any great import on whether the games were won or lost. We all wanted to win. It's always more fun to win. But I know it wasn't serious and intense. I think that's how everybody got."

The shellackings were now a weekly occurrence, and the injuries continued to mount. In a rematch against the Denver Gold on May 30, the Express dressed a total of 37 players, including only four defensive backs, three linebackers, and five defensive linemen. Following the 27-20 loss, the team was down to 35 semi-healthy players (including Young, who was still feeling the effects of his knee injury with a pinched nerve in his neck thrown in as an added bonus). The spate of injuries had become ridiculous. What went on during the Gold-Express game was even more so.

This is how nutty things eventually got in the Express' final days. Late in the fourth quarter of the football game, Don Klosterman summoned Herb Vincent to his private box in the Coliseum. Klosterman had an important request.

"I got word Mr. Klosterman wanted to see me. So I thought, What's wrong now? So I go up there and he wants me to put the Lakers-Celtics game on the big-screen television in the stadium, the DiamondVision, while our game is going on. It was the NBA Finals, and that's all the city was talking about anyway, so I said, 'Sure, why not?'

"As the teams would go into the huddle, they were watching the screen between their own plays to see what was going on in the game," Vincent adds. Young, a big basketball fan, wasn't about to miss any of the action as long as it was there for his viewing pleasure. Besides, Magic Johnson and Larry Bird doing their thing was far more interesting than what was taking place on the field. For the record, the Los Angeles Lakers defeated the Boston Celtics, 109-102, giving the few fans who did show up for the football game something to talk about on the ride home. Certainly nobody cared about the football game.

With only one Express home game remaining, new USFL commissioner Harry Usher, along with Klosterman, decided to hold the Express' June 15 game with the Arizona Outlaws at Pierce College in Woodland Hills, California. The Express were hoping to capitalize on the untapped San Fernando Valley market in a last-ditch effort to save the team. It was a desperate idea, and illustrated more than anything just how ludicrous things had become for the Los Angeles Express. After all, John Shepard Stadium didn't even have DiamondVision.

The playing of a professional football game in a junior college stadium said it all. Just when Young didn't think things could get any worse, he found himself on a bus headed toward Woodland Hills for a game in historic John Shepard Stadium. In typical Los Angeles Express fashion, the team couldn't even get to the game without incident.

Before leaving for the game, the bus driver, who hadn't been paid by the team for his services, refused to drive until he had some money in his hands. He wanted cash. Smart man.

Members of the equipment staff who had cashed their checks the previous day, paid the driver, and then the players pooled their money to repay them. The Express players assumed the bus driver would take care of the taxes himself. The cash seemed to appease the driver, and before long the bus was on the road.

For the game the Express carted in 10,000 temporary seats, expanding the stadium's seating capacity to a whopping 15,000. A sell-out was not only hoped for, it was expected. Tickets were only $5, and Klosterman figured a lot of people who didn't want to drive to the heart of L.A. for a football game would drive to Woodland Hills to see the Express play. He was wrong. Even with the reasonable ticket price, the interest simply wasn't there. A crowd estimated at 8,200 (the stadium had no turnstiles) watched the Express go down, 21-10. The fans who did go to the game saw a rare treat. Arizona's quarterback was Doug Williams. Los Angeles', of course, was Steve Young. After the game, Williams, surveyed the scene, and told the *Los Angeles Times*, "I thought I left all this when I left high school." Young's comment to the *Times* was even better. "I thought maybe the cheerleaders would decorate the team bus like they used to in high school."

The interview area was right outside the school buses. "We did the player interviews outside the locker room," recalls Vincent. "We were standing behind the buses with all that smell of smoke and oil burning off these horrible buses. In a way it was sick humor."

"That game was the ultimate slap in the face. We had to play our last home game in a junior college, and we couldn't even fill those stands," says Seurer.

By this time, Young's agent, Leigh Steinberg, was having intensive conversations with Tampa Bay. Steinberg was doing everything he could to ensure his client's future was in the NFL. Tampa Bay owner Hugh Culverhouse told Steinberg he would informally discuss Young's situation, but until the team received written permission from the rival league, the discussions wouldn't move into the next gear.

Only one game was left in the Express' 1985 season, and it required a cross-country journey to Orlando, Florida. With the season shot, and the 1986 season an impossibility, John Hadl wanted to showcase all his players (at least those who were still healthy), thus improving their chances of signing on with NFL teams. Hadl wasn't worried about Young. He knew he'd be playing somewhere. For a journeyman like Seurer, the future wasn't so certain, and Hadl figured every opportunity Seurer had to play would only help his chances of hooking on with an NFL club. For the finale, Hadl decided to give the quarterbacks equal time. Hadl told Young he'd play the first half, then give way to Seurer in the second. It was a decision that Young wholeheartedly supported. But when Seurer came in, as had been the case previously, Young didn't exactly enjoy standing on the sidelines doing nothing. Young paced. He wanted some action.

The Express went into the Orlando game with only 13 healthy offensive players. Depth wasn't in the team's vocabulary. The weakest area was offensive line, and Young knew he couldn't help there. He was courageous. He wasn't stupid. Running back was a different story. The team needed a healthy runner, and only Tony Boddie and Mel Gray were reasonably injury-free when the game began. That didn't last long. Behind a makeshift offensive line, both Boddie and Gray took a beating. By the third quarter, they were limping around and in need of a break. Young watched Hadl as the coach surveyed what he had left and decided all he could do was put in an offensive lineman at fullback to help block. Young intervened.

"Put me in, coach," Young said. He was serious. If there was one thing Young knew, it was how to run the football. Young convinced Hadl and checked into the Express backfield, just not in his usual position. In the huddle, Seurer was incredulous. He looked at Young, and Young stared back. It was the first time Young had played running back since that rainy, muddy day in his senior year of high school in the loss to Wilton High.

"That was weird. I was the quarterback and there was Steve playing running back. That's a rough position, running back. I don't think anybody really wanted Steve to do that. Steve had a long career ahead of him. But he asked if he could do it. That was something he wanted to do," says Seurer. "First of all it was a new challenge for him. That was the kind of guy he was too. He liked to find out what his limits were. He was just like a little kid. It was a new thing for him to do and he was, like, 'Hey, this will be fun. Let's try this.' He wasn't worried about getting hurt or any future considerations. It was a football game, and he enjoyed playing. He'd played quarterback so he tried running back. It was just something new for him to try and do."

Young was in for two plays before checking out of the game. He earned his pay by blocking. Hadl allowed himself to be talked into putting Young in as a running back. He wasn't about to call his number. The final Los Angeles Express game ever was a 17-10 loss with Steve Young doing time at fullback. Meanwhile, Steinberg kept the wheels in motion with Tampa Bay.

Young spoke to the *Orlando Sentinel* at the game's conclusion, knowing he had just played his last USFL game. "You can't keep this up, not the way things have been going for us. When you come to practice and moving vans are taking desks and stuff in the middle of the season, and then they announce that the team's folding the next week and then the commissioner shows up and says it was all just a joke . . . It's hard to go out and play football under those conditions," Young said. "I really don't know what I am going to do. I just know I can't go through anything like this again."

He wouldn't have to. As Young walked out of the
Citrus Bowl locker room after the 15th and final loss of a
most forgettable—some may argue unforgettable—season,
the Los Angeles Express and the USFL were in his rear-
view mirror, getting smaller and smaller.

CHAPTER ELEVEN

The Savior

On April 24, 1974, the National Football League awarded the city of Tampa, Florida, its 27th franchise. The Buccaneers began play in 1976 and went zero for that first, forgettable season, losing all 14 games. In 1977, the team lost an additional 12 to begin the year, running its streak to an NFL record 26, before finally breaking through with a win against New Orleans in the second-to-last game of the season. The dubious start, amazingly enough, was followed two seasons later by a run for the Super Bowl, an NFC Central Division championship, and a visit to the NFC Championship Game. The Bucs eventually finished one win short of the Super Bowl after a 9-0 loss to the Los Angeles Rams. There would be a couple more winning seasons to follow, but that was pretty much it for the team's upside. Through 1984, Tampa Bay's eighth NFL season, the club's won-lost record stood at 39-77-1. The franchise was pretty much a laughingstock.

And Steve Young desperately wanted to join this team.

In all his football-playing years, the only time a Steve Young team hadn't won consistently was that JV season at

Greenwich High and that final, forgettable year with the Express. Young considered himself a winner, a guy who was used to playing for winning teams. The 1985 Express season killed Young: The losing, the financial instability, the joke the team had become, everything. Young never wanted to experience anything like that again. He wanted to play in the NFL the way someone doing summer stock wants Broadway, and he suspected things would be a little better if he got that chance. He was partly right.

• • •

Almost immediately following the Express' swan song, speculation about Steve Young's football future began. In the middle of it was Leigh Steinberg, Young's agent, who was paid to take care of such matters. Midway through the 1985 USFL season, Steinberg began examining the details of the pact Young signed with the Express and J. William Oldenburg, hoping to find a clause that would allow his client to escape his Express contract. Young wanted out, and Steinberg wanted to accommodate his client. As he examined the document, Steinberg noticed a clause that prohibited Oldenburg from transferring Young's contract to another owner should Oldenburg decide to sell the team. When Oldenburg was forced out as Express owner before the 1985 USFL season, the league assumed financial responsibility of the Express, in essence becoming owner of the team. Steinberg had found his loophole.

On July 11, 1985, Steinberg, Young, Young's father, Grit, and USFL Commissioner Harry Usher met for more than three hours to discuss Young's future with the USFL.

Of course, Young had already decided there wasn't going to be a future. He wanted nothing more to do with the USFL or the Los Angeles Express. According to what Steinberg had told him, that would happen. He would be in the NFL. It was just going to take some time.

Usher was not pleased when Steinberg called the transfer of Express ownership from Oldenburg to the league a breach of Young's contract. He was incensed when Steinberg said Young was a free agent. Usher wasn't willing to allow Young to turn his back on his contract, and he wasn't about to make it easy on Young to just walk away from the Express. Usher wanted to keep Young in the fold. Usher thought the league was still viable and that it would survive. For that to happen, the commissioner needed players like Young to endorse the league and champion it like USFL bright lights Herschel Walker, Jim Kelly, Kelvin Bryant, and Anthony Carter were doing. Young wasn't about to do that. Usher began feeling Young slipping away.

Eight days after his initial meeting with Young, Usher reluctantly agreed to allow Steinberg to begin negotiations with Tampa Bay. The commissioner also played hardball. Usher told Steinberg he could negotiate on behalf of his client, he just couldn't sign anything without the USFL's permission. Usher also dropped hints that it would cost Young about $2 million to buy out his Express contract and sign with Tampa Bay. Steinberg called it a "king's ransom." Usher said Steinberg could call it anything he wanted. The verbal sparring went back and forth.

On August 9, as a public relations ploy, Usher announced how much Young had been paid for his two-years' service to the Express, trying to prove the USFL had upheld its end of the agreement Oldenburg struck with Young. In his press release, Usher said Young was paid $4.8 million for the 1984 and 1985 seasons, which included a $2.5 million signing bonus and $1.4 million settlement on an annuity to go along with his salary. Young and Steinberg couldn't disagree with Usher's announcement. Young was one of the highest-paid athletes in the country.

"I wish Young had the same venturesome pride in the USFL that Herschel Walker and Jim Kelly have shown. I like Steve personally, and at this stage, I'm sure there isn't time for him to come out blazing in the NFL," Usher told the *Los Angeles Times*. "We have a good shot at an L.A. franchise next year. It would help if he'd show Herschel's enthusiasm." Young wondered how enthusiastic Walker would be if he had to endure what Young had gone through with the Express.

Usher wasn't the only one taking shots at Young. New Jersey Generals' owner Donald Trump told the Associated Press, "Get rid of him. He's the most overrated player in football. I'd sue him for damages for not playing half this season." Trump was surely looking at the final 1985 quarterback statistics—where Young finished tied for 14th place among USFL quarterbacks—as the basis for his comments.

While the Steve Young issue was ongoing, Usher had other problems to worry about. The San Antonio Gunslingers had already released all of their players due to financial problems, and on July 31, after failing to meet their payroll demands, the Portland Breakers allowed the 39 players they had under contract to become free agents. The USFL was crumbling.

When Usher refused to drop his asking price of $2 million for a buyout, Steinberg told Usher he'd file a civil suit against the league and then allow the courts to interpret the validity of Young's contract. That was not what Steinberg wanted. Litigation could take months, and even if the court found in favor of Young, the quarterback would still be held hostage and, in all likelihood, miss the 1985 NFL season. No, Steinberg wanted a settlement. He just didn't want it to cost $2 million. Through it all, Young hardly seemed fazed. He assumed everything would work out, and that Steinberg would get him the best possible deal. Young was so relaxed that he went water skiing at Lake Tahoe with Gordon Hudson, then he attended the BYU-UCLA game at Cougar Stadium as negotiations heated up. In 1983, Young had started BYU's winning streak with the win over Bowling Green, and he never lost another college game. BYU then ran the board in 1984 on its way to the national championship while Young watched from the broadcast booth. A victory in the Kickoff Classic opened the 1985 BYU season, and the Cougars' winning streak had reached 25. Young continued to follow BYU with great interest, and he wasn't about to miss the BYU-UCLA rematch. To his horror, he was witness to BYU blowing a late lead and losing for the first time in more than two years. Although the game was the story, Young was a sidebar. After all, he'd started the winning streak and his presence at the game reminded fans of that fact. Everybody around Provo, including Young, was still very interested in what he was going to do.

With the football season in high gear, Young was impatient. He wanted to play. Not long after, things came together for Young. With Steinberg's threatened lawsuit against the USFL looming, Usher reluctantly dropped his "king's ransom" to that of a prince or maybe a squire, saying $1.2 million would free Young from his USFL contract. Steinberg wanted the USFL commissioner to go lower, but at least it was a compromise. Steinberg was satisfied and so was Usher, who issued this statement after the two sides acquiesced: "We felt it in the best interest of both the USFL and Steve Young that he should be released from his contract. Because of the Express' disappointing year, he has asked to be released. We have agreed to negotiate a buyout. He's an exciting player who was a credit to our league and we wish him well in his pro football future."

A little financial transaction resulted between Steinberg and Usher, after which Young was free to join the Tampa Bay Buccaneers. Before the NFL held its 1984 supplemental draft, then–Tampa Bay head coach John McKay flew to Los Angeles to watch Young play. McKay had decided he wanted to take Young with the first pick, and his trip to California only confirmed that choice. "I watched him and I thought, Here's the fastest guy on the field and he's white," McKay says. "I thought he was a great prospect. I've always thought if a quarterback could run that's certainly an advantage. So I came back and recommended to our personnel people that we take him. I was very impressed with him."

Although McKay retired following the 1984 NFL season, the decision-makers with the Bucs, including new head coach Leeman Bennett, felt Young was their quarterback of the future. Young had done nothing to cause Bennett and player personnel director Phil Krueger to feel otherwise when he traveled to Tampa and worked out for them. Young had an accurate throwing arm, and, yes, he was fast.

Steve DeBerg was Tampa Bay's incumbent signal caller, and he'd seen this all before. Too many times, in fact, and it was always the same scenario. Prodigy comes in and displaces veteran; veteran hangs around a while then packs his bags. That was the story of DeBerg's life. In San Francisco, DeBerg was benched when Joe Montana came on the scene. DeBerg moved to the Denver Broncos and did well until John Elway was signed. Back to the bench he went. Now in Tampa, DeBerg was about to be spurned for the third time, and this time Steve Young was the culprit. "Yeah, I felt kind of cursed. You just wouldn't think it could happen so many times," says DeBerg.

The day DeBerg was relegated to the bench was November 24, 1985, the day of Young's first start. But the stage was set September 10, 1985, when Young signed his second professional contract, this time a six-year deal worth $1 million per year. The Bucs held a press conference to announce Young's signing, only this gathering at One Buccaneer Place was on a slightly smaller scale than the soiree Oldenburg held when Young signed with Los Angeles. In other words, no hors d'oeuvres and no Orson Welles. The only interesting thing to come out of the press conference was Young's signing bonus, which amounted to $1 million and practically offset what it cost him to comb the Express out of his hair forever.

Young was a Tampa Bay Buccaneer. He was an NFL quarterback, just like Roger Staubach once was. He had finally arrived.

Whether Young liked it or not, he was perceived as Tampa Bay's savior. Fans expected Young to come in and singlehandedly turn the franchise's fortunes around. Bennett understood the expectations, and how impractical they were. That's why the coach sat down with Young after he had signed and talked to him about football being a team game, and how one player couldn't do it by himself. It was essentially the same talk John Hadl had with Young 18 months earlier.

"The fans expected him to be the guy and he wasn't quite ready. The expectations were very unrealistic, especially in that situation because there was very little talent to go with him. It just wasn't there. But there was no doubt in my mind about him, that someday he would be ready," says Bennett.

"He needed to learn how to be an NFL quarterback," says DeBerg, who could have been intimidated by Young's presence but wasn't. Of course, DeBerg was a veteran; Alan Risher, another USFL castaway who had signed with Tampa Bay before the '85 NFL season, was not. The Louisiana State product felt comfortable as DeBerg's backup, very happy with his situation as the team's number-two quarterback. With the addition of Young, Risher quickly became to the Bucs what Tom Ramsey was to the Los Angeles Express.

"I wasn't real happy to see Steve Young sign. I felt my job was being threatened, of course. When they signed Steve and gave him a pretty big chunk of money, I knew I was the odd man out," Risher remembers. "So, we weren't as chummy as maybe we got to be later on." When Young reported to work his first day as a Buc, he found his locker was situated between Risher's and DeBerg's, which somehow seemed appropriate.

"I made it in the NFL in the first place because Roger Staubach took me under his wing and explained things to me. He showed me what was going on. I wouldn't have ever made it in the NFL if he hadn't done that," says DeBerg. "So I always felt like since that's how I made it in the NFL to begin with, I should do the same thing. Plus, I always knew I was going to coach, so it was a form of helping and teaching the game of football. I never felt like it was to my disadvantage to help other quarterbacks. I guess I just felt secure in my ability to help the other quarterback."

One of the first things DeBerg did was sit down with Young and talk to him about the NFL and how to play quarterback against the greatest football players in the world. It was really the first time Young had a veteran quarterback who could be his mentor since Jim McMahon at BYU. Young was willing to listen. He relied heavily on DeBerg during those first few weeks in Tampa because quarterbacks coach Jimmy Raye had been knocked out of commission when he was hit by a car while jogging.

"We worked pretty good together. I remember I told him that to be a quarterback in the NFL, you have to be a pocket passer first even though you have the ability to scramble and do all those things. You're only going to be an outstanding quarterback in the NFL if you're a pocket passer first," says DeBerg.

After a while, Risher came around too, and became Young's closest friend in Tampa. Risher's wife was pregnant and living in Slidell, Louisiana, so Risher invited Young to move in with him. "He was just happy to get out of the USFL. I just think he was happy to get a chance to play somewhere," says Risher, who played a lot of golf with Young and even persuaded him to go to the dog track with him. Risher remembers Young having fun. He doesn't remember him putting any money down on the greyhounds.

As the two quarterbacks did more things together, Risher discovered that the Tampa Bay Steve Young was the same Steve Young who had played for the Express—the guy who would fish quarters out of his car's ashtray so he could buy burgers.

"We'd go somewhere and he'd say, 'Al, can you loan me five dollars?' And I'd look at him like, Are you out of your mind or what? He lived a $35,000-a-year lifestyle making a million dollars a year," Risher says.

Risher also remembers Thanksgiving 1985. Risher's wife had come to Tampa from Louisiana, and tight end Corwyn Aldredge and his wife were getting together with the Rishers for Thanksgiving dinner. Aware that Young was by himself with nowhere to go for the holiday, the Rishers invited Young to join their small celebration.

"We asked Steve to bring something to the dinner, and I think he brought a gallon of milk. We invited him over to eat, and he eats all the turkey and everything. Then when he leaves that night, he goes in the refrigerator and takes his half-gallon of milk with him. Stuff like that made you go, 'What in the hell is he doing?' We weren't offended, and we all just kind of laughed about it. It was more humorous than anything."

Chances are, Young had a lot on his mind. Earlier that week, Raye, back to full health, told Young that he was going to get his first start as an NFL quarterback. Fresh off a 62-28 thumping at the hands of the New York Jets, and sporting a 1-11 record, the Bucs needed a change. DeBerg had listened to the "We want Young. We want Young," chants that permeated through Tampa Stadium when things were going bad for the Bucs, which was often. So it wasn't much of a surprise to DeBerg when the fans finally got their wish.

"We never had a rivalry. We had a very healthy competition, and we both enjoyed competing. We were excellent friends, and I still consider Steve a real good friend," explains DeBerg. In that week before Young's first start, DeBerg worked closely with Young and made several suggestions for Young to consider. He told Young he needed to drop back and make the proper reads without watching the pass rush. "You have to feel the rush," DeBerg would say.

"Steve would actually look at the rush, and he was a good runner. But he was passing up a lot of successful plays if he'd have just kept his vision beyond the rush in making his reads. Sometimes his number-one receiver would be open and he was back there scrambling around. That was the one thing he needed to improve on," DeBerg recalls.

"Steve was better than a rookie in terms of the fact he had played some USFL games, but in terms of being prepared to play in an NFL game, he was raw. He survived basically on instincts. His inclination at that time was, when all else fails, run. He was a very good runner, and he still is. We didn't want to take that away from him, but we tried to minimize it. Obviously with him running around we were afraid of him geting hurt," says Raye.

With Young as the starter, Raye made some minor changes to the team's offense. He designed some things that would take advantage of Young's speed, including more bootlegs to get him away from the rush. "But we tried to make him stay in the pocket as much as possible," says Raye.

Tampa Stadium was a little more than half full for Young's first NFL start, and the crowd of 43,471 wasn't expecting much. They knew of Young's injury problems with Los Angeles earlier in the year. They also considered the plight of a rookie QB on a horrible team. Expectations, as low as the Buccaneers standing in the NFC Central, were only buoyed slightly by the sight of Young standing over center for the first time in a Tampa Bay uniform.

Young pretty much met the fans' expectations through three quarters of his first NFL start. The Bucs trailed 7-6 at halftime, and 13-6 after the third quarter. Young had thrown for 38 yards, and been sacked for minus-38 yards. It was a less than auspicious beginning. With 3:38 left in the game, and the team trailing 16-6, the Bucs' James Wilder scored on a six-yard run to bring them within a field goal. Then, Young took over. A defensive stand by the Tampa Bay defense put the ball back in Young's hands with 2:35 remaining. Young's first pass went 23 yards to Kevin House, then Young systematically drove the Bucs to Detroit's 19-yard line, where Donald Igwebuike kicked a game-tying field goal with a minute left.

In overtime, neither team came close to scoring until the Bucs took the ball at their own 39. Young hit Gerald Carter for a 19-yard completion, then scrambled for another five. With the ball on Detroit's 37, Wilder ran for 20 yards on five carries, moving the ball to the Lion 17. Young handed off three more times, all to Ron Springs, and the veteran running back got the ball to the six-yard line. Igwebuike was again called in and he split the uprights for a 19-16 win.

Young finished the day connecting on 16 of his 27 passes for 167 yards and no interceptions. He was also the team's second leading rusher. His 60 yards on the ground trailed only Wilder's 96. His healthy six-yard-per-run average was also impressive, although not nearly as much as this item: Young became the first Tampa Bay quarterback to lead his team to victory in his first start, something 13 other QBs before him hadn't done. Young had sat the bench the first 12 games of the 1985 Buccaneer season. Then it was his turn, and having been given a chance, he had done well. It was fun to play again, fun to win again. Young expected to be a Tampa Bay Buccaneer for a long time to come.

CHAPTER TWELVE

Your Tampa Bay Buccaneers

The Tampa Bay Buccaneers won only two games in the 1985 season, but Steve Young, in his four starts, guided his team to one of those two victories. When Young cleaned out his locker at the conclusion of the season in preparation for his return to Utah, he assumed he would be the starter when the 1986 season began.

Coach Leeman Bennett's philosophy when the Buccaneers fall camp opened—especially since the team was coming off a 2-14 year—was that nobody's job was safe. Bennett put every position up for grabs, with the quarterback derby getting the most attention. Young and Steve DeBerg would battle it out during two-a-days, with the winner emerging as the starter in the season opener at home against the San Francisco 49ers.

During the off-season, Young lived with Houston Oiler punter Lee Johnson, his old roomy from BYU. They decided that in the best interest of both of their careers, it would do them well to stay in shape. Young was prepared to work out during the off-season; he wasn't prepared for what Johnson had in mind. Every day the two would lift weights and run. They'd occasionally play pickup basketball at BYU's Smith Fieldhouse with other ex-BYU jocks, but the spring and summer weren't designed to be fun—at least not in Johnson's mind. He would remind Young of critics who said he had a weak arm, and goad his friend into working out longer and harder to strengthen his valuable left arm. Johnson never let up, which wasn't surprising to Young, who often referred to his buddy as "psycho" when it came to his workout theories. Before summer's end, Johnson fully expected Young to be in the best shape of his life, and that meant being the best-conditioned Buccaneer too.

When Young reported for Tampa Bay's preseason camp, he was the number-one QB. So far so good. Unfortunately for Young, that status didn't last long. Bennett had reservations about starting Young over the seasoned DeBerg, and it wasn't because of Young's supposed difficulty throwing the deep ball. During two-a-days, Bennett noticed Young was still playing like a rookie, struggling with the team's offense and having a difficult time picking up his secondary and tertiary receivers. He was also adding a few gray hairs to Bennett's head, which was nothing new for Young. He'd done it to Edwards and Hadl. Young's penchant for running the ball both thrilled and terrified Bennett. When Young made something happen with his running, it was great fun. But Young still played what Bennett called "helter-skelter" football. There was just too much freelancing for Bennett's liking. For that reason, Bennett named DeBerg the starting quarterback when the season began. It mystified the Buccaneer fans and the media who covered the team. Why go to the trouble of acquiring Young, sit him out for most of his first season, and then not give him a shot after getting that year of experience? That was the prevalent question in a lot of people's minds, Steve Young's included.

"We felt DeBerg gave us a better chance with his moxie and his years of experience. We just felt like we'd be better off with Steve DeBerg as our starting quarterback," recalls Bennett. "We wanted to start Young from the beginning. Of course we realized where we were from a standpoint of talent as a team, and we realized what we needed to do and what we needed for him to do. Rather than throw him out there and totally destroy his confidence, we felt we would be better off to bring him along slowly. There was very little talent to go with him. He really didn't have the cast around him that could take on a lot of the burden as far as winning and losing."

Says quarterbacks coach Jimmy Raye, "We did have an open competition, and Steve [DeBerg] won it on experience. He had better rapport with the guys. He had been there a couple of years and had done well, and I felt like the team rallied to him and felt a little more secure with him than they did with Steve Young because he had only played the last part of the year. Steve DeBerg was a guy who did it basically on preparation and knowledge. Steve Young was an ability player who, at that point, didn't know about the preparation required for that position."

Unfortunately for DeBerg, his ability to prepare for an opponent only took him so far. Against the 49ers in sultry 90-degree heat, 70-percent humidity in Tampa Stadium, DeBerg had probably his worst game as a professional. Although San Francisco only led 14-0 at halftime, DeBerg had thrown four interceptions, and at one point had completed more passes to the 49ers (four) than he had to his own team (three). In the third quarter, the interceptions continued. With eight minutes left in the third quarter, Steve Young began warming up on the Tampa Bay sideline. The 50,000-plus attending, who had been booing lustily after DeBerg's first interception, began the popular "We Want Young" chant. The yelling wouldn't sway Bennett into putting the backup in the game.

Though Tampa scored on a DeBerg 31-yard touchdown pass to Gerald Carter to cut San Francisco's lead in half, the Niners were in control of the game throughout, and Bennett saw no point to putting in Young in a situation where the team couldn't win. The chants continued and Bennett resisted. On the 49er side of the field, San Francisco coach Bill Walsh was surprised Bennett stuck with DeBerg. Walsh couldn't understand why Bennett wouldn't put in someone with Young's gamebreaking speed to force the 49ers to change their defensive scheme a little. Walsh was grateful for his good fortune, and thankful to have Joe Montana. The Niner quarterback had missed three weeks of the preseason with a sprained ankle, but showed no ill-effects by completing 32 of his 46 passes for 356 yards in the rout.

On the sidelines, an amazed Young watched the precision of Montana specifically and the 49er offense as a whole. The way San Francisco ran its offense reminded Young of his senior year at BYU when the Cougars were successful at whatever they tried. Young also noticed that after a seven-interception, 18-for-40 passing performance in the blowout loss, his team was looking strangely reminiscent of some UTEP teams he played against at BYU.

It was an ugly start to a season that would get progressively more ugly, and more frustrating for Young. In week two against the Minnesota Vikings, Young got his second "Did Not Play" in the box score, and the Vikings got a relatively easy 23-10 win. DeBerg threw two more interceptions against the Vikes, and finally Bennett had seen enough. The ability guy was coming in from the bullpen to start against the Detroit Lions in the Silverdome. Helter skelter or not.

Maybe it was the fact Young drove that Detroit-made Oldsmobile for so many years. Whatever, Young had success against the Lions. The better explanation was that Detroit was as bad as the Bucs. With Young as the starting QB, the Bucs beat the Lions in 1985, and they would do it again under a similar scenario in 1986. What was strange about the 1986 game is that statistically, Young stunk up the joint. He completed only 6 of his 15 passes for a mere 39 yards, and he rushed for just 24. But one of those rushes resulted in a touchdown and the Bucs had their first win of the season. The thing Young brought to each game was an excitement sorely missing in Tampa Bay. Players seemed to respond to Young's ability to rally his team to play at a higher level.

"He was so competitive. He was trying so hard and trying to get everybody to have the same energy for the game that he had," says Raye, who called the plays for Tampa Bay.

Who knows what might have happened to this Tampa Bay team had it started a winning streak after the Detroit game. Maybe things would have turned out differently. It wasn't too much of a fantasy to imagine the Bucs with a 3-2 record after game five, based on their performances.

After the win in Detroit, Tampa Bay returned home to host the Atlanta Falcons, who spoiled the plan by beating the Bucs in overtime, 23-20. It was a gut-wrenching loss too. Tampa Bay appeared to have the thing won until Falcon kicker Mick Luckhurst kicked the game-tying field goal with no time left in regulation. The kick was set up by a Young interception. Luckhurst then booted the game winner, another 34-yarder, with only 2:25 left in overtime.

The following week on the road against the Los Angeles Rams was a similar story. The Rams and Bucs played to a standstill through regulation. But in overtime, the Rams' Eric Dickerson peeled off a 42-yard touchdown run to lift them to the win. Instead of being 3-2, Tampa Bay was 1-4 and in the early stages of rigor mortis.

Recalls Raye, "We had a lot of guys who, with the playoffs probably out of the question, were just getting through the year. I know it was extremely difficult for a young guy like Steve, who had been involved in winning programs and had been successful, to have to deal with that."

In a three-week period, the Tampa Bay Buccaneers started rotting. By week 16, they were to the core, leaving Young in a situation that was just as bad, and maybe worse, than his final year with the Los Angeles Express. Where the players had banded together in Los Angeles, dissension was prevalent with the Bucs. Backbiting, finger pointing, and general discontent pervaded the residents of One Buccaneer Place and Tampa Stadium. If Young thought that final season with the Express was tough to stomach, the 1986 version of the Tampa Bay Buccaneers was the equivalent of food poisoning and a Christmas fruitcake chaser.

"Anytime you're losing like that the mood is not good. You begin to doubt yourself, and when you doubt yourself we all know it's hard to do anything," says Bennett. "By the same token, all these guys were 21 to 30 years old, give or take a couple of years, and they've looked at a lot of football film and they can see whether the talent's there or not there. And it just wasn't there."

It wasn't rare for Young to overhear teammates talking about how much they wanted the season to end, and what their off-season plans were. For whatever reason, there was a tradition of losing at Tampa Bay. No matter what Young did to change it, he couldn't overcome it by himself. He gave it the old college try, and all he got was an A for effort.

Case in point: Against the St. Louis Cardinals, Young passed for 260 yards and one touchdown while rushing for another 47. He accounted for 307 of Tampa Bay's 347 yards of total offense. The Bucs lost, 30-19.

Tampa Bay was a team in turmoil. Rumors about Bennett's job security became food for discussion, and a transaction on October 20 didn't endear the team to the Tampa Bay faithful, or unfaithful as the situation began dictating. The day after a 38-7 loss to New Orleans, the Bucs waived former all-pro tight end Jimmie Giles, running back Ron Springs, and wide receiver Kevin House in a move that angered many longtime Buccaneer fans. The injuries also added up. In a four-week period between games 7 and 11, the Bucs were forced to make 21 roster moves. By season's end, there were 16 first-year NFL players (10 rookies and six USFL refugees) playing for Tampa Bay. While the Los Angeles Express claimed to have assembled the best young football team ever, this aggregation of players was merely one of the worst young football teams ever.

The Bucs played in conditions that would have been difficult for any franchise, which explains why Tampa Bay rarely won. The second and final win of the 1986 season came in a showdown between two former USFL quarterbacks, Young and Jim Kelly of the Buffalo Bills. Statistically, Kelly was better, hitting on 29 of his 39 passes for 342 yards. Young was a credible 14 of 24 for 193 yards. Kelly also outrushed Young 42 yards to 32 yards, but Young had two touchdown runs and the Bucs had a 34-28 shootout win. It marked the only time all season Tampa Bay scored more than 25 points in any game.

For the final home game of the season, in a battle of the Bays, Green beat Tampa, 21-7, with only 30,099, the third smallest crowd in franchise history, watching. Fans tossed lemons onto the field to show their displeasure over the bill of goods the Bucs were trying to pawn off on them. An essential part of being a Tampa Bay fan was frequent trips to the produce department. The Tampa Bay Buccaneers were spiraling downhill fast, ready to reach their nadir. If it hadn't come during the lemon-tossing episode, then it came at Disney World in Orlando.

At a Christmas booster club meeting following the Green Bay game, one Tampa Bay player, guard Sean Farrell, decided he wasn't going to giftwrap the comments he had prepared for the gathering. What Farrell had to say was a huge lump of coal for the franchise.

"I know what I want for Christmas," he began. "I want to get the hell out of Tampa Bay. I don't care where I'm going. I just want out."

Although the situations were different, the 1986 Tampa Bay Buccaneers were the Los Angeles Express revisited. Thirty-thousand fans at an NFL game was the equivalent of 10,000 in the USFL. Steve Young had no trouble picturing any of his former Express teammates saying what Farrell said. He was thinking the same thing.

It was safe to say that Tampa Bay was not the type of franchise Young was looking for when he bought his way out of the USFL. Trading the Los Angeles Express for the Tampa Bay Bucs was tantamount to the kid on the playground swapping a liverwurst sandwich for his buddy's kippered fish snacks.

To a man, the Tampa Bay Buccaneers wanted to be put out of their misery. That happened four days before Christmas against the St. Louis Cardinals. All the 21-17 loss to the Cards did for Tampa Bay was ensure it of the number-one pick in the 1987 NFL draft.

In 1984, Tampa Bay owned the first pick, but traded it to the Cincinnati Bengals in exchange for quarterback Jack Thompson. That deal was an abject failure. Had the trade never happened, and the Bucs not dealt the pick, they might have been the team, instead of the Bengals, trying to persuade Young to play in the NFL instead of jumping to the USFL.

Buccaneer management evidently learned from its mistake. The Bucs were not going to trade the top pick in 1987, and they were going to do what hindsight told them they should have done three years earlier. They were going to use the pick to draft the best college quarterback available.

CHAPTER THIRTEEN

If You're Going to San Francisco

For two years Steve Young had been playing the game looking through the earhole of his helmet. The Bucs were a mess, and football from their point of view was often skewed. They had less talent than any team in the league, and hope of getting better seemed remote. Worse than that, many of the players didn't seem to care whether they won or not. Young could deal with losses; he couldn't deal with apathy.

Young would get knocked silly by angry linemen every game. When his helmet wasn't being turned sideways, his body was. Such was life with the hopeless, hapless, don't ever go chinstrap-less, Tampa Bay Bucs. Young had been given two years to resurrect the franchise, and in his 19 games as Tampa Bay's starter he'd gone 3-16. That wasn't going to cut it.

It was mainly the 16 losses that explained why Steve Young was forced to experience something that was as foreign to him as Donald Igwebuike. Young was falling out of favor with the fans, the media, and most importantly, the Tampa Bay decision makers. Even Coach Leeman Bennett's support of Young had wavered, but that hardly mattered. Everybody knew Bennett was as good as gone as the Bucs' coach, and that Young would probably follow him out the door. In the Christmas shopping spirit, Tampa Bay was having a clearance sale on quarterback Steve Young, suddenly available to the highest bidder.

Oh, it wasn't that obvious. Young still attended the team's minicamp in February with new head coach Ray Perkins, and was still considered the team's number-one quarterback—at least in name—all through camp. But, the Bucs held the first pick in the 1987 NFL draft, and Perkins made no secret who he intended to select. Before being fired, Bennett had said the same thing. The Bucs were going to draft Heisman Trophy winner Vinny Testaverde, the University of Miami quarterback. Testaverde's five interceptions in a loss to Penn State in the Fiesta Bowl had, in part, cost the Hurricanes the national championship. When asked about Tampa Bay's possible drafting of Testaverde, Young bluntly said he could not see himself coexisting with Testaverde, and that he expected to be traded should the Heisman winner join the club.

The year prior, Tampa Bay also had the draft's number-one pick, and used it to select Auburn running back and Heisman Trophy winner Bo Jackson. Bo knew he didn't want to play football for Tampa Bay. So, Jackson opted for a baseball career and the Buccaneers opted for tears. The Bucs might as well have picked Beau Bridges for all the good the Bo Jackson pick did. The franchise had lost credibility around the league and with their own fans, making the 1987 draft an important stepping stone for the Bucs.

During the Testaverde hype, Young never demanded a trade. He figured a trade, if it was going to happen, would take care of itself. For a team with as many needs as the Bucs, it seemed improbable that they could afford to draft Testaverde and keep Young. Not long after taking the Tampa Bay job, Perkins began sending out trade feelers for the former 40 Million Dollar Man. The pocket was closing on Steve Young.

This whole process with Buc management gave Young a better appreciation for what Eric Krzmarzick, Mark Haugo, and Gym Kimball at BYU, Tom Ramsey and Frank Seurer with the Los Angeles Express, and Steve DeBerg and Alan Risher with the Bucs had gone through. They were each relegated to the bench when Young came along. Like an old roll of adhesive tape, this time it was Young being tossed aside.

The turmoil with Tampa Bay fit perfectly into the Steve Young storyline at the time. In the early spring of 1987 Young's life was one interception after another. The Bucs had fired Leeman Bennett, Young had called off his marriage to fiancee Gwen Goodson the night before the two were to tie the knot, and with Vinny Testaverde in the fray, Young's football future was as nebulous as his love life.

In Utah, Young stayed patient and tried not to worry about what was happening. He told his agent Leigh Steinberg that he'd prefer to play in a warm-weather city on a team that could contend. He was talking about San Francisco.

The idea of going to the 49ers wasn't immediately an attractive option for Young. He was well aware of Joe Montana and what he had done for the franchise. Although Montana had proven over the previous two years that he was somewhat fragile, the prospect of sitting behind Montana waiting his turn was unsettling to

Young. His entire thought process changed after a discussion with Steve DeBerg.

When it became clear the Bucs were going after Testaverde, DeBerg took Young aside and told him if he had an opportunity to go to San Francisco, he should take it. DeBerg was speaking from experience, having learned a lot in his early years in the league from Bill Walsh. DeBerg told Young the best quarterback coaching was in San Francisco, and that the 49ers would be the best team he could play for. Young changed his stance. The Montana situation bothered Young, but not enough to dissuade him from making his desires known to Perkins.

Steinberg explained to Young that he could make those suggestions, but he was really at the Bucs' mercy. They could trade Young to whoever and for whatever they wanted. And without a no-trade clause in his contract Young had no leverage. Perkins did tell Steinberg he would try to meet Young's requests as he began negotiating with other general managers and coaches around the league. The fact remained, though, that Perkins wasn't in the business of trying to make Steve Young happy. Fortunately for Young, Hugh Culverhouse was. Tampa Bay's owner, who had done so much to try to get Young to join the Bucs in 1985 by promising the quarterback he would be the club's foundation, felt an obligation to Young. Culverhouse was willing to accept a lesser package in trade to satiate Young's desires. Yes, guilt definitely figured into the equation, so when Young said his first choice was to play for the San Francisco 49ers, Culverhouse told Perkins to do his best to accommodate Young.

When the Bucs put Young on the trading block, right there lining up at Perkins' door was San Francisco 49er coach and general manager, Bill Walsh. A year earlier, Walsh inquired about the availability of Steve Young. Bennett laughed off Walsh's request, telling his counterpart in San Francisco he wasn't interested. "I got a lot of those kinds of calls," says Bennett. "I never paid much attention to them because I wasn't going to trade Steve Young."

Having been spurned by Bennett in his attempts to acquire Young a year earlier, Walsh decided to test the waters with Perkins, who, Walsh knew, wasn't as enamored of Young as Bennett had been. He was also aware of Culverhouse's altruistic intentions.

It was only logical that Walsh would want Young in a Niner uniform. Walsh had a long-time relationship with BYU head coach LaVell Edwards, the two having traded notes off and on over the years. Both coaches espoused the passing game, and the two offenses were quite similar, using a progressive reading system that put a premium on a quarterback who could make decisions and then execute them. When Walsh needed a new quarterback coach in 1986, he went to Provo and plucked Mike Holmgren from Edwards' staff with Edwards' blessing. Throughout the years Edwards had observed many 49er practices, and Walsh had done the same at BYU. Young had even had the chance to rub shoulders with Walsh, who attended some BYU spring practices and later spoke at a BYU banquet during Young's junior year in college. In that speech in April of 1982, Walsh said, "Two of the most important things I look for in an athlete coming into the 49er program are intelligence and success in the classroom." Walsh might as well have added "a lefthander who can run" to that sentence because, however unwitting he was at the time, Walsh was describing Steve Young.

The thought of being reunited with Holmgren, the college quarterback coach he had always gotten along with, appealed to Young. With former Cougars Tom Holmoe and Todd Shell already on the 49ers' roster, the addition of Young to the team made San Francisco look like BYU West.

• • •

San Francisco 49er quarterback Joe Montana, who had led his team to its first Super Bowl championship during the 1982 season, and then repeated the feat in 1984, was not doing well physically. He'd struggled in 1985, and hadn't looked particularly sharp as the 1986 season began. Montana was suffering from back trouble that forced him to miss a week of practice and the September 10 game against the Los Angeles Rams in Anaheim. The Niners fell to the Rams, 16-13, with backup quarterback Jeff Kemp subbing for Montana.

Unable to make any headway in his attempt to pry Young away from the Buccaneers, Walsh directed his attention to Jim Everett, the unsigned number-one draft choice of the Houston Oilers. Walsh wanted Everett, and the 49ers offered two first-round draft picks and defensive lineman Manu Tuiasosopo for the former Purdue Boilermaker. A week after the San Francisco-Los Angeles game, it was the Rams, not the Niners, who won the Jim Everett sweepstakes. Houston demanded all-pro nose tackle Michael Carter instead of Tuiasosopo, and Walsh waved goodbye. He didn't want Everett that much. Walsh had stepped to the plate twice in a year in his attempt to get a frontline quarterback and had swung and missed both times.

Walsh was always worried about Joe Montana's health, but it was by no means a dire situation when Everett went to the 49ers' rival. Nobody at the time knew of the severity of Montana's back troubles. Everybody found out soon enough. The San Francisco quarterback situation became desperate when the team announced Montana would undergo surgery on September 15 to remove a herniated spinal disc from his lower back that was pressing against the sciatic nerve. Doctors estimated the recovery time at anywhere from 12 to 14 weeks, essentially knocking him out for the season. The docs were off by a month. On November 9, Montana returned to the lineup for a 43-17 stomping of the St. Louis Cardinals that added to his legend. Montana was supposed to have trouble walking after the surgery and here he was playing and shredding the Cardinals. He'd pulled another rabbit from his hat.

Montana always despised the word brittle when people talked about him, but it was becoming an appropriate adjective and noun, despite his uncanny ability to bounce back from each injury. Walsh was concerned that the rigors of an excessive preseason, a 16-game regular season, and the playoffs, would be too much for Montana and his ailing back. If that was the case, Walsh was hardly confident Jeff Kemp or Mike Moroski could step in and run the Niner offense like nothing had happened.

The injuries continued to mount for Montana. The back held up; his noggin didn't. In the playoffs against the New York Giants, the 49ers were steamrolled, 49-3. The scary part came when Montana lay on the Giants Stadium turf for 10 minutes before being loaded into an ambulance. New York lineman Jim Burt hit Montana so hard that Joe ended his season with a concussion. The rest of the day, Montana, in street clothes, complained of double vision and a headache. He was also having trouble staying awake, and it wasn't because the game was boring, which, by the way, it was.

• • •

The Bucs and 49ers began preparing for 1987, with the 49ers staying apprised of Young's apparently tenuous situation with Tampa Bay. It seemed half the league was doing the same thing. Showing varying degrees of interest in the soon-to-be erstwhile Tampa Bay quarterback were the Pittsburgh Steelers, the Atlanta Falcons, the Dallas Cowboys, the St. Louis Cardinals, the Los Angeles Raiders, the Green Bay Packers, and the San Diego Chargers.

The number of clubs showing interest in Young should have been indication that he was still highly valued around the league. But that didn't matter to the Bucs. They had gotten caught up in the Testaverde hoopla in Florida, and decided early on that he was Tampa Bay's quarterback of the future.

Young's life in central Florida was over. He had gone to Tampa for the team's mini-camp in February, and quickly returned to his new home in Park City, Utah, at its conclusion.

As during his days with the Express, Young could be gone at a moment's notice. The only tie he had to Tampa was a contract, and all appearances indicated the four years and $3.2 million left on his deal would be assumed by another team.

On April 3, three weeks before the NFL draft, the Bucs announced the signing of Testaverde, whose selection on draft day would be a formality. These were heady times for a franchise in pretty bad shape. Ray

Perkins had a good reputation around the league from his days coaching the New York Giants and the University of Alabama. Testaverde, like Young previously, had been given the title "savior," and owner Hugh Culverhouse was being more generous with Testaverde than he had been with Young, which was saying something. Testaverde signed a six-year deal worth $8.2 million, including a $2 million signing bonus and $4.1 million in deferred salary.

Young had been pushed aside. Even 3,000 miles away in Utah, Young was not oblivious to what was happening with the Bucs. But what could he do? He'd accepted the fact the Bucs thought more of Testaverde than they did him. That wasn't easy for Young, but he was dealing with it. From his Park City home, which, incidentally, was his most extravagant purchase since turning pro, Young told Steinberg to call when he heard some news. Otherwise, he'd just assume he was still a member of the Tampa Bay Buccaneers. Young wasn't about to sit around and stew about his future. He was back in the dating loop after his failed engagement to Goodson, and some healing was going to have to take place. The two had been an item since college, and she had been there for Young during the tumultuous signing of the Los Angeles Express contract. Now Young was available, and he made it clear it was incumbent of his friends to help him meet girls. That task was left to Jim Herrmann and Lee Johnson. The trio would also hang out at Young's new house, and they'd play a lot of golf. In other words, Young was on summer vacation.

NFL general managers and coaches, especially Steve Young suitors, were not. They all worked on deals that could free Young from Tampa Bay, and they would occasionally travel to Utah, interrupting Young's vacation to have him throw passes and run sprints. Bill Walsh was among those who journeyed to Provo on more than one occasion to evaluate Young. He expected to be impressed and he was. But on April 18, Walsh became skeptical about his ability to make a deal for Young. Perkins was demanding first- and third-round picks from the 49ers in the upcoming draft, a price far too steep for a team that was essentially trading for a backup quarterback. Walsh didn't look at Young as merely a backup, although he told Perkins that in an effort to keep Tampa Bay's asking price down. In Walsh's mind, Young was not only a walking, talking insurance policy, but he was potentially the 49ers' quarterback of the future. But the likelihood of Young ever putting on a 49er uniform looked extremely remote when Perkins laid his offer on the table. Two high picks were way in excess of what the 49ers could or wanted to give up, so Walsh simply backed off. Perkins was demanding the same from St. Louis, Green Bay, and Dallas, the other teams who remained interested in Young. Like the 49ers, the Cardinals, Packers, and Cowboys were all suffering from sticker shock.

Had Perkins been acting alone, Young would have gone to the Packers, the team willing to part with higher draft choices than the other three. But with Culverhouse calling most of the shots, it wasn't that black and white. When the 49ers didn't bite on Perkins' demands, he dropped the price. Walsh reentered the picture. For second- and fourth-round picks in the 1987 draft, Young could be had. The Cowboys pushed hard, essentially offering the same thing. But the Cowboys were a team in a slow downward spiral, and Young wanted to play for a franchise that had a chance to go to the Super Bowl.

For the 49ers, keeping their number-one draft choice was imperative. With it, they could still have a shot at drafting the player they really wanted, Harris Barton, an offensive tackle from North Carolina and the consensus best offensive lineman in the draft. If they could get Young and Barton, the draft would be a success, regardless of what they did in the subsequent rounds.

When Walsh and Perkins reached an agreement, the Buccaneer coach called Steinberg, who, in turn, called his client.

The phone call to Young came on April 24. Predictably, Young had just gotten off the golf course.

"Steve, you're going to San Francisco," Steinberg told him.

The first thoughts that jumped into Young's mind were Bill Walsh and Joe Montana. Young couldn't have been happier. One minute he was a member of one of the worst-run franchises in the NFL and the next he was with one of the league's best.

It seemed like an ordinary pre-draft football trade. There were many in the NFL who figured Young was destined to be a backup the rest of his career. In Young's four years in professional football, he'd been extremely unspectacular. Nobody was questioning his running ability and the excitement he brought to any given game. The knock was whether he could be a traditional drop-back NFL quarterback. The old lines about the strength of Young's arm, and whether he could lead a team to a title, resurfaced. Whispers even began that Young was nothing more than a high-priced bust.

In the annals of professional sports, the Steve Young-to-San Francisco trade will go down as one of the great steals of all time. Only nobody knew it at the time. Just as Young's collegiate path was paved when Doug Scovil quit his job at BYU, this trade did the same thing for Young's professional career.

Perkins' statement to the media after the trade was congenial. "I have a lot of respect for Steve. Not that he's a great player because he hasn't proven that yet. But I think he's a great person." Perkins also indicated San Francisco's offer was the best of the three Tampa Bay considered. That was Perkins' way of saying he had accomplished what Culverhouse had requested while saving face, his own and the franchise's, at the same time.

Through the team's media relations department, Hugh Culverhouse released a statement. "I want to thank Steve for the great contributions he made to the Buccaneers. He gave us much enthusiasm and displayed the true colors of a real competitor. We wish him well and believe he'll have a fine career with the 49ers."

CHAPTER FOURTEEN

The Waiting

It came with some irony that Steve Young would want to join the San Francisco 49ers. After all, as a college senior, he resisted going to the Cincinnati Bengals because he didn't want to have to ride the bench behind Ken Anderson, who happened to be a Bill Walsh-taught quarterback. Four years later, Young was elated at the prospect of being a backup to a Bill Walsh-taught quarterback named Joe Montana. Young could have gone just about anywhere, but he wanted San Francisco.

If there's one thing Young needed in his football career in 1987, it was stability. There had been none in Los Angeles, and, despite solid ownership, Tampa Bay was a mess on and off the field. Once the trade to San Francisco became a reality, there was a vapor trail out of Park City toward the Bay Area. Young couldn't wait to begin preparing for the season. His golf game would have to wait.

Joe Montana was vacationing in Italy when he was notified the club had traded for Steve Young. It was news that didn't leave the veteran quarterback with feelings one way or the other. Montana's back was in good shape, and he expected business as usual once the season began. He certainly wasn't threatened by the addition of Young to the Niners' roster. Montana looked at Young as just another backup quarterback to flash him signals from the sideline. There was no reason to think of him any other way. In Europe, Montana heard his coach's quote, "We fully expect Joe to continue as the leader and the mainstay of our team."

That's what Walsh told the media after the trade, but it wasn't quite what Walsh told Young privately. When the coach and his new quarterback spoke, Walsh told Young he had plans for him to be the team's quarterback of the '90s, and that he couldn't forsee Montana playing many more years because of the rash of injuries taking a toll on his body. In his own mind, Walsh gave Montana three years—tops—before he'd have to call it a career. Hearing those words from Walsh gave Young plenty of reasons to rejoice. He could bide his time.

San Francisco's acquisition of Young was applauded for many reasons: It hadn't cost the 49ers much to get him away from Tampa Bay, Young was still young at only 25, and he was more than just a clipboard-toting backup. The trade, most observers agreed, was a good one for the 49ers. Disconcerting to a lot of Niner fans were the rumors that the 49ers put the beloved Joe Montana on the trading block after dealing for Young. Although the 49ers denied that Montana was ever available, there were nagging reports that the Pittsburgh Steelers were very interested in the quarterback who grew up in Monongahela, Pennsylvania, near the Steel City, and that Walsh and 49er owner Edward DeBartolo Jr. listened and carefully considered what the Steelers were offering.

With Young in the fold, the Montana trade stories did and didn't make sense. In Young, the 49ers had a competent quarterback to take over for the fragile Montana. But San Francisco also had, in Young, a guy who would be forced into immediate action had Montana been traded. Playing immediately for a team with one of the most complicated offenses in the league would be no easy trick.

It was all a moot point when Montana wasn't traded. Steve Young had no intention of going to San Francisco to sit on the bench for any great length of time. That was certain. Conversely, Joe Montana wasn't about to simply step aside and let somebody take his job.

There was no quarterback controversy with the San Francisco 49ers in April of 1987. However by the end of the year, there would be.

• • •

Much like he did when he reported to Los Angeles and Tampa Bay, Young immersed himself in the 49er playbook and with the coaches who would teach him the system, specifically quarterbacks coach Mike Holmgren. This was Young's way of trying to learn things the 49er way as quickly and as well as possible while deprogramming from his mind everything he'd been taught at Tampa Bay.

The reunion with Holmgren was a comfortable one. Young knew how Holmgren thought and coached, and Holmgren found Young to be the same excitable, eager quarterback he'd coached at BYU. Young treated his early 49er days in much the same way he did as a freshman at BYU. Back then, Young would watch Jim McMahon and try to pick up his tendencies and figure out why he did certain things. In San Francisco, Young scrutinized the working relationship Montana had with his coaches and how he reacted to their coaching. He would also listen carefully to the questions Montana asked in position meetings with Holmgren, and wonder why. On the field, Young tried to replicate what Montana did in certain situations. Sometimes it worked and other times it didn't.

Young would get his first chance with the 49ers in the Hall of Fame Game in Canton, Ohio, against the Kansas City Chiefs. Walsh was also extremely interested in what Steve Young, a giant question mark to the rest of the league, could do.

In the preseason game against the Chiefs, Walsh made it easy on Young, letting him take his first official snap as a San Francisco 49er quarterback from the Kansas City eight-yard line. On the previous play, Montana had been popped in the chest hard, and was removed from the game. Within striking distance of the end zone, Walsh delivered room service to Young. From point-blank range, Walsh knew Young would have a good chance of getting the team in the end zone, and more importantly, would gain some much-needed confidence. It didn't work out the way it was planned. Young's third-down pass fell incomplete, and although the 49ers scored on a fourth-down play, Young hadn't done much to further the drive.

Montana came back in the game on the next possession and marched the Niners down the field like he'd done before being knocked out. Like the last drive, with San Francisco knocking on the Chiefs' door, Young was inserted back in the game. With the ball on Kansas City's 19, Young was anything but stellar. He couldn't get the 49ers into the end zone, taking a sack and throwing an incompletion that was almost intercepted. Montana watched from the bench. He didn't say anything but was upset he had been pulled in the middle of a drive. His drive.

Young was given every chance to excel in the exhibition season. Not only did Walsh want to evaluate Young and give him some experience, Montana was hurt more than he wanted to admit against the Chiefs. He strained ligaments in his sternum, which paved the way for Young to start against the Los Angeles Raiders. Against the Raiders, Young spiced up the game with several runs that kept the Los Angeles defense off balance all night. As had become his trademark wherever he played, Young would not hook slide before a tackle. Fans seemed to take to the quarterback who ran like a running back. Young accounted for 308 yards of total offense to the Raiders' 192.

That was fine for the preseason. What really counted, though, was the 16-game regular season schedule. When the season started for real, Young was behind Montana. Neither quarterback was surprised by this. But, Young wasn't happy about it.

"He was just frustrated. He was miserable. He couldn't stand it," says former tight end John Frank who shared an apartment with Young in Los Gatos. "I liked him because he was pretty clean cut. It was a lot of clean living and I respected that and liked that. But he was very overbearing to live with sometimes because he wasn't playing."

The frustration was similar to that difficult first year at BYU. Young would be discouraged and he'd call his father in Connecticut for advice. Steve would complain about being stuck behind Montana, and Grit would tell him to quit whining.

"You've got the best job in America," Grit said. "Look at how much money you're making and all you're doing is signaling plays in. How hard is that?" That pretty much ended the conversation even though it did nothing to assuage Steve's frustration. That would be there as long as he wasn't playing. When he would play was anybody's guess, but Walsh's decision.

Several questions remained: Could Joe Montana stay injury-free? Could the team come back from the embarrassing 49-3 pummelling against the New York Giants in the playoffs and make another run at the Super Bowl? Most 49er watchers figured Montana was the key. If he could get back to Super Bowl form, they had a chance. If Montana went down, few held much hope that Young, an NFL neophyte, could lead the team to the glory they had become accustomed to since Montana and Walsh began their synergy together.

All systems were go until the 24-day players' strike brought things to a grinding halt. Young and Montana were out, and Mark Stevens, a scab quarterback who had played for the University of Utah, was in. In the games between replacement players, Walsh scrapped the vaunted 49er passing offense and implemented—yes!—the wishbone. In their first scab game, Stevens and the 49ers were a rousing success playing the New York Giants on Monday Night Football. The revenge leveled against New York wasn't very sweet for San Francisco since none of the players masquerading as 49ers and Giants had played in the '86 championship game. It was fun for Walsh to show up Giant Coach Bill Parcells on national television, though, as the 49ers totally destroyed the New York Giant scab players.

By the time the strike was settled, all the players were ready to get back to work. The strike hadn't wrecked the season, and only one regular season game was lost to the walkout. Young tried to stay sharp during the three-week layoff, knowing nothing had changed with the 49er quarterback situation. Montana was still Montana, the best quarterback in the game when healthy. That was the qualifier, though. Montana had to be healthy, and history had shown he couldn't finish a season that way. December 14 proved that.

The ABC Monday Night Football crew was in San Francisco along with the Chicago Bears for what many were saying was an NFC Championship Game preview between teams that had won two of the last three Super Bowls. For good measure, the 49ers and Bears sported league-best 10-2 records.

Monday Night Football was no new thing to the San Francisco 49ers. It was, however, to Steve Young. He toiled for two seasons in Tampa Bay and never had the opportunity to play before the national audience that makes MNF games so unique. None of his games at BYU were on national network television, and although the Los Angeles Express were on all the time, who was watching football on TV in June? Especially USFL football?

This late-season game was a big deal to both teams in their attempts to prove supremacy as they prepared for the playoffs. For Young, it figured to be another week working on his hand signals.

A Candlestick Park record crowd of 63,509 turned out to see the game, and ended up getting to watch the B team. Bears quarterback Jim McMahon did not play because of a pulled hamstring, and early in the first quarter a pulled hamstring of his own sent Montana to the showers. That meant the two quarterbacks from the 1982 Holiday Bowl, Steve Young and Mike Tomczak, would duke it out the rest of the night. It wasn't much of a fight.

Young's first play from scrimmage was a quarterback keeper around the left side that he turned into an 18-yard gain. That was an old trick Young used. At the beginning of any game, Young was always nervous. This game was no different. To combat the butterflies, Young would jump into the fray by calling his own number. That's what the 18-yarder did for him against the Bears. It also endeared him to the crowd, who liked his courage when he didn't slide.

After that, it was almost ridiculous how easily the 49ers took apart the Bears. Young threw a career-high four touchdown passes, and the 41-0 slaughter left the Niners in good spirits, despite Montana's injury and the loss of linebacker Keena Turner to a sprained knee. The 49ers improved to 11-2. They had the NFL's best record, and probably the best backup quarterback in the league.

Walsh could only smile after the game. He had worked so hard to get Young into a 49er uniform for nights like this one. The team hadn't skipped a beat with Young at quarterback; all systems were go. Walsh hadn't earned the title "Genius" for nothing.

• • •

Nobody was calling for Young to start over Montana. People were just grateful there was a high-quality quarterback playing behind the future Hall of Famer. A lot of those sentiments changed in the 49ers' first playoff game, a sloppy, muddy Candlestick Park battle against the wild-card entry Minnesota Vikings.

The Vikings came, they saw, and they surgically dismembered the San Francisco defense, while putting the hurt on the vaunted Niner offense. With still half of the second quarter to be played, the Vikings led 20-3, mainly because Joe Montana had been horrible. With 7:36 remaining in the first half, Montana had completed only 5 of his 12 tosses for a paltry 58 yards. Another one of his completions, this one to Minnesota defensive back Reggie Rutland, went for 45 yards and a touchdown in the wrong direction. The fans didn't boo Montana. They were too stunned.

The 1987 season wasn't supposed to end like this. The 49ers were destined to roll to their third Super Bowl title and become to the 1980s what the Green Bay Packers were to the 1960s and the Pittsburgh Steelers were to the '70s. They weren't supposed to fold up like some cheap road map, at home, no less.

The quarterback who had led San Francisco to so many end-of-the-game comeback wins would not have a chance to do anything of the kind in this one. In the locker room at halftime, Bill Walsh considered pulling his quarterback and letting Young do what he could for the entire second half. After consulting with Holmgren, Walsh decided to let Montana start the third quarter. He'd give him another chance. In two possessions, Montana played six downs. The team didn't get a first down and punted both times. Montana was totally ineffective.

As Montana reached the bench after that second series, Walsh walked over to him and said, "I'm going with Steve."

For the first time in his career, Montana was being benched.

211

While Walsh did his best to put Young in preseason games in situations where he could succeed, the situation against the Vikings was hardly ideal. Entering the game with the 49ers trailing 27-10, Young was like a general dispatched to Little Big Horn to clean up after Custer.

Comfortably ahead, Minnesota coach Jerry Burns felt his insides churn a little when Young began moving the 49ers. His first pass, a 31-yarder to fullback Roger Craig, took San Francisco to Minnesota's four-yard line. Young finished it from there, running for a touchdown to cut the deficit to 10. The crowd was back into it. The San Francisco offense no longer looked like 11 flatliners. Now, the defense had to get a stop and the momentum might carry the Niners from there.

It wasn't to be. Minnesota got a field goal to make it 30-17, then curiously, Walsh called for kicker Ray Wersching to attempt a 48-yard field goal instead of going for a first down after the Niners had moved the ball fairly well on their next possession. When Wersching's kick fell short, so did any thoughts of a 49er rally. It was all over for the 49ers, but in a way it was just beginning.

Young played so well that he now became a problem for Bill Walsh. The backup quarterback was good enough—12 for 17 in the passing department for 158 yards, one touchdown, and a team-high 72 yards on the ground—that questions about the efficacy of Joe Montana began. Was Montana being phased out? Was Young the team's new number-one quarterback? After all, when it was time for a patented Joe Montana miracle against the Vikings, the master of the two-minute offense sat on the bench. Walsh cited a need to change the chemistry as the reason for the switch to Young, but that didn't go over well with at least one 49er. After Walsh inserted Young into the game, wide receiver Dwight Clark, who, as it turned out, was playing his last game, approached Walsh and let him have it. Clark wasn't one to back down from a situation where he felt strongly, and he knew he had to say something in defense of his friend. Clark wanted Walsh to know he thought the coach had publicly humiliated Montana, and given up on him too early.

Nobody associated with the 49ers was very happy with the way the season ended. Some were just a little more upset than others. Young was delighted at the chance to play meaningful minutes in an important game. Montana was angry about being replaced. And Walsh had an entire offseason to deal with the situation.

Let the controversy begin.

CHAPTER FIFTEEN

Quarterback Controversy

Joe Montana's dismal performance against the Minnesota Vikings might have been more galling to the followers of San Francisco 49ers' football had it not been for everything he had done earlier in the season. Before the 1987 season began, many around the NFL were suggesting Joe Montana was either on the downward slope of his career, or already finished. To everybody's surprise, Montana's surgically repaired back held up, he led the league in touchdown passes (31), and his 102.1 quarterback rating topped the league. The 49ers' 13-2 record in the strike-shortened season was also a league-best. Unfortunately, playoff flameouts were becoming too commonplace. Since winning Super Bowl XIX, the 49ers had been knocked from the playoffs three consecutive times without giving the Super Bowl so much as a sniff. In all three losses, the offense had been the problem. Montana's performance and subsequent defeat at the hands of the Vikings in '87 wasn't just one loss, but the third indictment that maybe Montana no longer had the magic. It even sounded like Walsh was preparing for the worst. The only people firmly behind Montana were 49er fans, who still embraced the Bay

Area demigod as much as ever. If anything, Steve Young was perceived as an interloper trying to horn in on Montana's sacred turf.

To avoid any sort of quarterback controversy, all 49er coach Bill Walsh had to do was name Montana the starter for the 1988 season and be firm about it. The Young-Montana mano a mano could be a small kitchen fire. Instead, Walsh let it become an inferno that threatened the entire house. And at least some of the time, Walsh himself was fanning the flames.

In the days following the loss to Minnesota, Walsh was, at best, coy about his intentions with his two quarterbacks. He wouldn't commit to either, saying only that the job was up for grabs and that Young and Montana would be in open competition come training camp.

Walsh knew his plan could backfire, but he was convinced not naming a starter would make Steve Young a better quarterback. Walsh was also quite certain it would motivate Montana into proving he did indeed have something left. When the young quarterback from Notre Dame battled the veteran in 1980, it was Montana, the Golden Domer, who beat out Steve DeBerg for the 49er quarterbacking job. In 1988, Walsh wanted to find out if Montana could still beat out his challenger with the roles reversed.

The two protagonists would be at minicamp, but the real battle would take place in July. They would both have the next six months off. But neither guy would be relaxing.

Young was encouraged by what was happening. He had played in seven games in his first year with San Francisco, starting three. Things had shaped up the way Walsh said they might when he wrested Young away from Tampa Bay. Young returned to Utah after the

Minnesota loss thinking he had no worse than a 50-50 chance of being named the starter for the 49ers' 1988 season.

• • •

Since graduating from BYU in 1984, law school had always been in Steve's plans. Grit Young had said that his oldest son's profession as a football player wasn't really work, and that he wouldn't be making an honest living until he got a "real" job. If Young was ever going to do what his dad had said, he knew he would do it as an attorney, like his father.

Young checked out BYU's J. Reuben Clark Law School to see how he could play professional football and attend law school at the same time. It wouldn't be easy. His only option was to enroll in winter semester classes that began in January and plan on taking five or six years to get his juris doctorate. With BYU's law school not offering summer semester, Young would have one three-month window each year to take classes. That window, he decided, would begin in January of 1989.

Meantime, football would take precedence. Young felt, as did Montana and Walsh, that the 1988 NFL season would be a critical one for the 49ers' offense, whoever was at the controls. Young just hoped it would be him.

In the preseason, the 49ers, in their own rich-get-richer way, had an enviable problem. They had two quality quarterbacks playing a position where only one could be a starter. Some tough decisions had to be made. Should they invest in the future and go with the youngster, or do they start the guy who had done it so many times before? It was a dilemma any coach would like to have.

217

As 49er camp began, it seemed Walsh was leaning toward Young. At least that's what appearances indicated. Montana wasn't his usual sharp self, and rumors continued to dog the team. The previous year there was speculation the 49ers were willing to deal Montana if the right offer came. One year later, the same type of story reared its head. The hottest rumor had Montana going to the San Diego Chargers for two San Diego first-round draft picks and running back Gary Anderson. The deal purportedly fell through when Walsh demanded linebacker Billy Ray Smith instead of Anderson. The rumor was another blow to Montana's ego, even though, as had been the case before, Walsh and owner Eddie DeBartolo denied most of the story. They did confirm that there had been talks, but it was the Chargers who had approached them about making the trade. DeBartolo insisted the 49ers had absolutely no interest in trading Joe Montana.

Walsh proved his boss' claim by naming Joe Montana the 49ers' starting quarterback to begin the season. Maybe Bill Walsh had Montana pegged as the starter all along, and maybe the quarterback controversy was nothing more than a smokescreen. The coach's motives weren't clear. But by the season opener against the Saints in New Orleans, Young was back in his traditional spot on the sidelines while Joe Cool was taking the snaps when the games started for real.

Montana was back, the 49ers were picked to contend for the Super Bowl, and Walsh seemed happy with his choice. Then he became wishy-washy. Walsh named Montana the starter against New Orleans to open the season with a caveat; Young would start against the New York Giants in the second game.

Although nobody was using the word, it looked strangely like a platoon system, with Walsh resembling a baseball manager taking full advantage of a quality bullpen in the late innings. In the second half of the Giants game, Walsh benched Young largely because of two Young fumbles. He sent Montana in to save the day, which he did by throwing a 78-yard bomb to Jerry Rice with 42 seconds left in the game. It was vintage Montana making the kind of play that seemed to indicate all was well. It wasn't. The flip-flopping of quarterbacks was atypical Bill Walsh behavior and was adversely affecting Young and Montana. Both quarterbacks wanted the starting job outright, and both felt they deserved it. Walsh's platoon was quickly becoming a divisive influence on the team, and danger signs were everywhere despite the 49ers' 2-0 start.

Montana started the 49ers' home debut against the Atlanta Falcons. Walsh promised playing time to Young, but that didn't happen. Montana went the distance; he threw for 343 yards, and completed 67 percent of his passes. He also tossed three interceptions as the Niners went down hard, 34-17.

It was a curious decision not to play Young, especially in light of two things: Montana was clearly off his game, and Walsh, without being prodded by reporters, said Young *would* play.

The controversy was heating up as Young and Montana cooled personally toward one another. The on-field competition was strictly professional but feelings were beginning to get in the way.

"I don't think the controversy amounted to much until Steve really threatened Joe's job. When Steve threatened the position, then there was a conflict," says John Frank, Young's roommate.

In post-game comments, Montana said he was tentative against the Falcons with Young "lurking" on the sidelines. Montana made it sound like Steve Young was Lon Chaney or Bela Lugosi. Montana also intimated that Walsh was slowly phasing him out of the offense and slowly integrating Steve Young. Montana was frustrated and it showed on the field, his play looking strangely reminiscent of his spontaneous combustion against Minnesota in the playoffs.

The platoon wasn't easy for Young, either. He wasn't always comfortable playing for Walsh, and had a tendency to press when he did play because he didn't always know when he'd play again. It was a case of trying to prove as much as he could in as little time as possible. In an interview with the *Los Angeles Times*, Young talked about playing for Bill Walsh.

"Walsh doesn't talk a lot to quarterbacks. I think he expects perfection, and you know that, and he drives you to play well enough just to get a nod. You think you're playing pretty well, and it's like, ah, I think he nodded at me. I think I almost saw some reaction. I take that as positive. He somehow gets you on edge. You feel you're always on edge. I get the feeling he's staring at me every play, you know, and I'm saying, 'OK, I'll do better. I promise.' I think he's driven me by whatever he's done. Or maybe I've just imagined it, but I keep working hard. Trying to impress him, I think, is the ultimate goal."

In many ways, Young wanted to please Bill Walsh the same way he wanted to please his own father. Both were demanding men who expected a lot.

In week nine of the 1988 season, Young pleased his coach in a most unusual way.

At a Candlestick Park rematch with the Minnesota Vikings, Young got the start and was as bad in the first half as Montana had been the last time these two teams met. He completed only 4 of 11 passing attempts and the Niners trailed 7-3 at halftime. The game was Young's to win or lose, however, as Montana was sitting this one out with a bad back.

Things got better for Young in the second half. Much better. He directed a 97-yard touchdown drive, and he hit John Taylor with a 78-yard scoring pass to bring San Francisco to the precipice of victory. It still appeared it wouldn't be enough as the 49ers trailed 21-17 with a little more than two minutes to play and the ball on the Viking 49.

The play sent in from the sideline was for receiver Mike Wilson to go across the middle on a hook play. As Young dropped back, all he saw was Minnesota lineman Chris Doleman's hand go up. Without waiting for something else to develop, Young tucked the ball under his arm and took off. He said later he was trying to find tight end Brent Jones, but Young seemed more intent on running than throwing the ball. Good thing. The first Viking with a shot at Young was safety Joey Browner. Swing and a miss. Lineman Keith Millard was next, followed by safety Brad Edwards and linebacker Chris Martin. All three grabbed for jersey but came up with air. Nobody could bring down Young, who by this point looked like a pinball bouncing off the bumpers. The crowd was screaming as Young kept his legs churning. The 20, the 15, the 10, the five. Young's legs turned to rubber and he began losing his balance.

As his center of gravity got lower and lower, Young dove for the end zone before anybody else could lay a hand on him. The crowd was stunned, delirious. It was the kind of run that would be shown over and over and over. The kind of play that makes ESPN rich. It was Willie Mays robbing Vic Wertz in center field, or Michael Jordan switching hands in midair. This was play-of-the-day, play-of-the-year material. The most amazing part of Young's run was that there was no hint it might be coming. Two other San Francisco fourth-quarter possessions had bogged down before Young's late-game heroics.

Young had gotten the Niners out of a nasty mess, a mess he created by his poor play in the first half. He earned NFC Offensive Player of the Week honors, mainly because of the run and because he completed 10 of 15 passes in the second half. Six years later, as the National Football League celebrated its 75th anniversary, Young's catch-me-if-you-can scramble was voted the top run in the history of the league. Not a run by Jim Brown, O.J. Simpson, Walter Payton, or Red Grange, but a run by Steve Young.

In the locker room, center Randy Cross told the *San Francisco Chronicle*, "Steve's running style mirrors his personality. He's intense, churning, aggressive. If Joe was in that situation, he'd be cool and calculated. I'd hesitate to apply those words to Steve Young. He's not a cool and calculated surgeon. He's the last guy I'd want to operate on me, especially if he's in a hurry. He's very intense, very hurried for a quarterback. He looked like he was about to die of a heart attack going into the end zone. It was extremely ugly, but the final spasm was all he needed to get in."

Believe it or not, Cross was being complimentary of his teammate, the anti-Montana.

Young's run could have solidified his claim on the job. A good showing the following week against the Phoenix Cardinals, in a game to be played on DeBartolo's birthday, almost certainly would have accomplished that. Instead, Young watched a 23-0 lead evaporate into a 24-23 loss. It was his mistake with 1:38 left in the game that killed the Niners. With the Cardinals out of timeouts, Young ran out of bounds and stopped the clock. That would haunt Young the rest of the season as the Cardinals came back to score the winning touchdown moments later.

Montana, who was receiving cortisone shots for his ailing back, was given a clean bill of health and returned to the lineup for a home game against the Raiders. Walsh said the only reason Montana was starting was because he was healthy, not because he was upset with Young's botched play late in the Phoenix game. Young felt otherwise, despite Walsh's pleas to the contrary.

"When Joe is healthy, he is our starter. That was his status going into the season, and continues to be. The only people who have questioned it have been some of the local press. It's up to me to decide whether it's in his best interest to play extensively," Walsh said after his decision to start Montana.

The return of Montana did not inspire the lackluster 49ers. Against the Raiders, a team San Francisco pounded in the preseason, Montana couldn't get his team in the end zone, something that hadn't happened to a 49er team in Candlestick Park since 1981. Maybe that should have been an omen. 1981 was Montana's breakthrough year, and 1988 would be his comeback year.

Even with the poor showing by Montana and the team, the 6-5 record and the distinct possiblity the Niners would miss the playoffs, Walsh went with Montana for a Monday night game against Washington. In his previous five games, Montana had one touchdown pass. Against the Redskins, Montana threw 18- and 80-yard touchdown passes. He was back. So was his back. He was 15 of 23 for 218 yards in the 37-21 victory that jumpstarted the team in a way nobody anticipated. The reemergence of Montana relegated Young to his normal role as a high-priced insurance policy. Chapter One of the 49er quarterback saga was over, and Montana was the clear winner.

CHAPTER SIXTEEN

Joe Cool

The San Francisco 49ers took possession of the ball on their own eight-yard line. Three minutes and ten seconds remained in Super Bowl XXIII, and the Cincinnati Bengals led the 49ers, 16-13. The Bengals had just capped an 11-play, 46-yard drive with a Jim Breech field goal to break a 13-13 tie. After the kick sailed through the uprights, all eyes fell on Joe Montana, who seemed to saunter onto the field without a care in the world. All Steve Young could do was stand on the sideline and watch. Young had a hunch what might be coming.

All season, people were suggesting that Montana was done as an NFL quarterback and that he should gracefully step aside for Young. Then the end-of-the-season run that led into the playoffs began, and the 49ers rode their quarterback as far as he could take them. Montana wasn't ready to retire, and in the waning moments of the Super Bowl he had his chance to prove it once and for all.

• • •

The first half of Super Bowl XXIII had easily been one of the worst halves of football in Super Bowl history. The two teams were tied at 3-3, and fumbles, missed field goals, penalties, and general ineptitude gave this game a preseason feel. The poor play of the first half eventually gave way to scintillating second-half drama.

After a season full of injuries to Montana, Young tried to stay mentally sharp during his first Super Bowl, knowing full well he might be put into the game at any time. The call never came. Standing on the sideline, even if it was the Super Bowl, was not Young's idea of a good time. Everybody else, it seemed, was having all the fun. Lee Johnson, the Bengals' punter and Young's best friend, got off a 63-yard punt in the second quarter that set a Super Bowl record, and another friend, Cincinnati defensive end Jason Buck, was also playing a lot, harassing Montana. The fact Young was watching the Cincinnati Bengals, the team that probably would have drafted him had he not opted for the Los Angeles Express, also was not lost on him. When Young went to the Express in 1984, the Bengals drafted Maryland quarterback Boomer Esiason as their quarterback of the future. Four seasons later, Ken Anderson, the quarterback Young didn't want to sit behind, was retired and Esiason was starting in the Super Bowl. The whole situation wouldn't have been so hard to accept if Young had been on the field. He wasn't, and there lay the conflict.

• • •

On first down, Montana hit Roger Craig for eight yards. Then he hit tight end John Frank for seven more. Jerry Rice caught a seven-yarder, and Craig picked up a hard-fought yard on a sweep. It was obvious what Bill Walsh was doing. He wasn't going for the win on one play. He was going to chip away at the 92 yards the team needed, and he had Montana to carve up the defense.

Dink to Craig. Dink to Frank. Dink to Rice. Dink. Dink. Dink. That was the 49er offense.

The drive that would eventually become known as "The Drive" was going well. But suddenly, Montana was hyperventilating, and looked panicked. He wanted to call a timeout. Walsh said no. So Montana intentionally threw the ball away with 1:22 on the clock. On the next play, Rice broke past two defenders for a 27-yard gain that moved the ball to the 18, and a Montana to Craig pass took San Francisco to the Cincinnati 10 with 39 seconds left. Win or lose, San Francisco was treating the huge, worldwide audience to the kind of finish no Super Bowl had ever had before. Montana called timeout.

In the huddle on the sideline, Walsh called the play "20 Halfback Curl, X Up," where Rice, the decoy, goes in motion and wide receiver John Taylor sets up all the way to the left. The play is designed for Rice to receive double coverage in the left side of the end zone, springing Taylor, who is supposed to run a simple post pattern to the inside. It worked. Montana found Taylor and the Vince Lombardi Trophy once again belonged to San Francisco.

Jerry Rice, with 11 catches for 215 yards, was named the game's most valuable player. But Montana got most of the accolades for his engineering of the drive that won the world championship for the 49ers. With three Super Bowl titles to his credit, Montana personified the quarterback who could do it in the clutch. He was the apotheosis of his position.

Without warning Steve Young was suddenly a forgotten man, just another backup quarterback in a league full of them. It was a hard pill for Young to swallow, especially since he knew there were plenty of teams in the league for whom he could start.

• • •

Young couldn't have selected a worse year to begin law school. Reaching the Super Bowl extended the season to late January. When Young finally made his way to Provo he was already three weeks behind. In the quarterback derby with Montana, he felt farther behind than that, and appearances indicated Young wouldn't have a whole lot to look forward to in the 1989 season. Montana was the 49ers' starting quarterback. This point was made abundantly clear when Bill Walsh retired a few days after the Super Bowl and his replacement as 49er head coach, defensive coordinator George Seifert, immediately put a lid on any quarterback controversy talk. It was a no-brainer for Seifert, who saw what Montana did during the final weeks of the season and in the playoffs.

Seifert also understood what Young was going through. In discussions between the two, Seifert equated Young's situation with his own, reminding Young that he had toiled for many years as an NFL assistant with the hope that one day he'd become a head coach. He told Young to be patient.

Young was plenty used to that.

CHAPTER SEVENTEEN

Back to the Bench

When Bill Barber injured his shoulder prior to the 1978 Greenwich High School football season, Steve Young stepped in, grabbed the job, and never looked back.

Young would leave Greenwich and show a modicum of patience at each of his next stops until the coach gave him the keys to the car. That's the way it was with BYU, the Los Angeles Express, and the Tampa Bay Buccaneers.

In San Francisco it was different. No matter what Young did, no matter how many times it looked like he would be given the starting quarterback job, Joe Montana would show up and reclaim the throne. To Young, Montana was both the Energizer bunny and Jason from the *Friday the 13th* movies. The guy would not go away.

During the 1989 season, Young said of Montana, "He's the quarterback who won't die. Joe's obviously outlasted my expectations, and maybe his own." You could almost hear the sigh. In 1987, Walsh told Young he thought Montana had three years before retirement. How was Young supposed to know Walsh would step aside before Montana?

Young was in his third season with the 49ers, and he was as close to being named the team's starting quarterback as he was to winning a Super Bowl with Tampa Bay. Montana seemed to be defying logic, getting better as the days and years progressed. Never was that more apparent than in 1989. Whereas the Niners' 10-6 regular season record in the 1988 Super Bowl year was very mediocre, their 14-2 mark a year later topped the league. Montana was positively magnificient, the team dominating. Young played a role in the team's success, minor as it was. It had become a standard part of the 49ers' operation that Young would play when needed. But in the end, he'd always have to make way for Montana. The team still belonged to Joe.

In a game against New England played at Stanford Stadium in Palo Alto, California, because of damage to Candlestick Park by the San Francisco earthquake, Montana suffered a sprained knee in the first half. Young came in, completed 11 of 12 passes (a new team completion record, 91.7 percent), and threw three touchdowns in a 37-20 win. That's the way it was for Young. He'd play and play well when called upon. But as soon as Montana returned, Young was back on the bench wearing a baseball cap.

On November 12 against Atlanta, Montana started, completed 16 of 19 passes for 270 yards and three TDs in a 45-3 win. The Niners were a machine, rolling over and through all comers. The days of Montana looking tentative in the pocket were long gone. His performances suggested Montana was playing a game of "Anything You Can Do, I Can Do Better."

The least surprising aspect of the season came when Montana and company routed the Denver Broncos, 55-10, in Super Bowl XXIV. Montana was brilliant in a game that was never close. He threw a Super Bowl record five touchdowns, completed 13 straight passes at one juncture, and walked away with his third Super Bowl MVP trophy and his second consecutive NFL MVP award.

George Seifert said, "He's probably the greatest quarterback ever to play this game." Young couldn't disagree. "He's not looking up at anyone," he said.

Young now owned two Super Bowl rings, and neither one meant much to him. It was nice to be part of such a great team and organization, and nice to have gone to two Super Bowls. Compared with the USFL or Tampa Bay, San Francisco was heaven. But Young didn't feel like he'd contributed much to the cause. He had played in four-and-a-half games in '89, and compiled a 120.4 quarterback rating to Montana's 112.4. His outstanding play prompted Young to tell *San Francisco Chronicle* writer Ira Miller before the 1990 season that he was overqualified to play backup to Joe Montana. "If I thought I was just barely qualified, it might not be a big deal, but I feel very overqualified." Who could argue? Maybe Steve Young wasn't Joe Montana. But he wasn't Babe Laufenberg either.

For that reason, Young was in high demand by the NFL's quarterback-poor teams, the proletariat to the 49ers' aristocracy. By 1990's NFL draft, it was Young, not Montana, who was being discussed in the NFL rumor mill. There was no substantiation to any of the trade rumors involving Young, and, in fact, the 49ers had no intention of letting Young go anywhere except to law school. That's where Mike Holmgren tracked Young

231

down. He flew to Utah to meet with his number-two quarterback and assure him of his status with the team. Holmgren's words were comforting to an extent. Young knew the team needed him, just not enough to make him the starter. Leigh Steinberg, Young's agent, strongly suggested his client ask the team for a trade to a team where he could play full time. Each time the subject was broached, Young refused to think about it. He'd invested three years of his life with the 49ers, time, no matter how frustrating, that was well spent. To walk away wasn't in Young's plans.

So he prepared for another season of sitting, another season of frustration. Montana started the 1990 season and the Niners looked very much like a team with every intention of winning its third straight Super Bowl. While Young saw considerable action in each of his first three years with the Niners, he hardly played in 1990, only attempting 62 passes. In contrast, Montana was an iron man, attempting 520. The Niners went 14-2, crushed Washington in their first playoff game, and were one step away from the Super Bowl. Then Leonard Marshall ended it all. With 9:41 to play in the NFC Championship Game against the New York Giants in Candlestick Park, Marshall barrelled into Montana and made him eat grass.

The scene looked hauntingly familiar. One frequent image of Montana was Joe standing with both arms raised after throwing a touchdown pass. But there was another image, the one of him crumpled on the turf in pain, just like he was after being leveled by Marshall. The hit knocked Montana from the game. He had a broken finger in his throwing hand and a severely bruised sternum.

The backup came on to try to do something against the Giant defense. Down two at 15-13, Young took his team on a drive, a clock-consuming, yardage-eating drive. The Niners needed a field goal for Young to get his chance to start in the Super Bowl.

Then Roger Craig—sure-handed, clutch fullback Roger Craig—fumbled the ball and the season away as New York recovered. Young had been denied again. As he dejectedly walked off the Candlestick Park turf, Young was crushed. He had been so close and it slipped away. With six months for Montana to heal, Young figured that next season he'd be handed the clipboard and that would be that.

But Young didn't know about the soreness in Joe Montana's right elbow.

CHAPTER EIGHTEEN

Taking the Reins

It was lonely standing there in the rain, doing what he'd done so many Sunday afternoons while waiting to play. The Prodigal Son had returned, the Bay Area rejoiced, and Steve Young again felt like an outsider on his own team.

With the nation watching, Joe Montana made his triumphant return to the 49ers in a meaningless Monday night game against the Detroit Lions. Montana, who hadn't taken a snap in a game since Leonard Marshall KO'd him almost two years earlier, was again on the Candlestick Park turf trying to recapture the magic of Super Bowl seasons past. Young was back on the sideline.

The deal had been set well before game time. San Francisco was assured of a first-round playoff bye, so 49er Coach George Seifert decided to play Young in the first half and Montana in the second. Everyone—Seifert, owner Edward DeBartolo Jr., team president Carmen Policy—agreed; this would be a good way for the club to evaluate Montana's progress, while showcasing him for other teams who might be interested in trading for him. Playing Montana would also give him one last chance to strut his stuff before the home folks.

When Montana entered the game, the roar was deafening. Signs welcoming Montana were everywhere. Young tried to look comfortable on the sideline but clearly wasn't. How could he be? How could he compete against Montana's legend? He'd gone 12 of 18 for 153 yards in his two quarters of work, securing his second consecutive NFL passing title in the process. Of his six incompletions, three were dropped passes. He was the only QB in league history to surpass 100 on the rating chart in two successive seasons, and he was on his way to the league most valuable player award. But on this night, nobody seemed to care about Young. His stint against the Lions was a formality, the warmup act for what the 55,907 fans who jammed Candlestick really came to see. They wanted to see if the guy who had undergone nine different surgeries in his career still had it. Chants of "Joe. Joe. Joe," echoed through the rainy, windy stadium. In the stands, Joe lovers wore replicas of Montana's scarlet number-16 jersey. There weren't many number eights.

It was a perfect situation for Montana. The Lions were on their way to a 5-11 season, and they had mailed their season in by halftime. Montana could have been Joe Piscarcik and still done okay. He began slowly, feeling his way through the third quarter, looking a lot like a guy who hadn't played in 700-plus days. Then he kicked it into gear and began doing what the fans had come to see. Montana led the 49ers to 17 points on back-to-back-to-back drives, with one touchdown to tight end Brent Jones causing ABC's Dan Dierdorf to say, "All is right in the world again."

The hype was gushing out of the ABC booth. Fortunately for Young, he wasn't near a television.

When the game ended, Montana left the field to the cheers of the crowd. Young turned down a chance to go to the post-game press conference, choosing instead to answer questions in front of his locker. "It was a great tribute to Joe, and I was excited to be a part of that," he said diplomatically, trying not to sound hurt. He slowly dressed and made his way to the players' parking lot.

The usual gathering place for Steve Young and his friends after a home game is Chili's in San Bruno. It's typically a low-key get-together. Young talks about the game, people swap stories, and everybody goes home happy, especially after a win. With all the hoopla surrounding Montana's return, this was not a typical night.

As Young drove to the restaurant, he listened to a call-in show on his car radio. The question of the night was, "Should Steve Young start in the playoffs for the 49ers or should Joe Montana be given the nod?" Young knew what the results would be before the station began accepting calls. No one would have blamed Young had he called it a night after the game and just picked up Burger King on his way home. But 50 of Young's friends from the Bay Area and Utah had gathered to be with their friend, and Young wanted to be with them. Chili's it was.

Entering the restaurant, Young was probably more magnanimous than he should have been. Nobody was sure what kind of mood he would be in, considering everything that had happened at the game, but Young ended all doubts. He greeted his friends, and talked to everybody at the table. He could have brooded but he didn't. He worked the room. He picked up the tab. He made a lot of people happy.

• • •

Steve Young became the 49ers' starting quarterback for good in the 1991 season when doctors surgically reattached a torn tendon in Montana's right elbow in October of that year. The surgery would shelve Montana for the entire season. But he didn't plan on being out for all but two quarters of 1992, as well.

Young took over the 49ers. At first, he was loaned the team until Montana got better. Young's hold on the position became more permanent when Montana's recovery took longer than anticipated. For Young, it was a bumpy two-year ride. In his first year as starter, the Niners went 10-6 and missed the playoffs. His record as a starting quarterback was even worse. San Francisco was only 5-5 in games Young started. When Young went down with an injury, backup quarterback Steve Bono came in and the team went 5-1. A new controversy began. Bono was Montana's best friend on the team, he played like Montana, and after years of mimicking his buddy, Bono even resembled the legendary quarterback when he'd drop back to pass. So although Young won the league passing title, his debut had been a flop in the eyes of Niner fans. Even when Young pronounced himself healthy, Seifert stayed with Bono while Young watched. Holding a player out even after the player wasn't injured anymore was something Bill Walsh had done with Joe Montana to give Young some playing time. Now Young was putting up with the same tactic, with Bono the chief beneficiary.

The fact that Joe Montana did not like Steve Young didn't help matters. Montana had resented Young ever since Bill Walsh opened up the job after the Minnesota playoff loss in 1987. Montana was annoyed that Walsh took an immediate shine to Young, and did, at least in Montana's mind, as much as possible to acclimate Young to the team and the 49ers' system. Montana also wasn't used to a quarterback who was extremely talented and ambitious. Montana's caddies during his years in San Francisco were journeymen quarterbacks like Jeff Kemp, Mike Moroski, and Matt Cavanaugh, players who hardly threatened Montana's status. Montana spoke openly and nastily about Young to the *Washington Post.* "Steve is on a big push for himself. And any time you have a competition, there is a certain amount of animosity. I can say we have only a working relationship. That's all it is. He's on my team, but as far as I'm concerned, he's part of the opposition. He wants what I have."

About Montana, Young's comments were typically benign. "In 1991 Joe wasn't very helpful. But there was a transition time. People weren't sure what they were supposed to say, how they were supposed to react. Joe's very competitive, and I don't know any other way to be. We do very well considering we're very competitive. People think there are fist fights in the back room. That's not the case at all."

No, just icy silence. For two players whose lockers were so close, they rarely had much to say to one another. Montana sulked in 1992 when the Niners named Young the starting quarterback, telling friends and teammates how he had been betrayed by the organization he had done so much for. Montana wasn't willing to admit that Young had passed him on the depth chart, and he was going to do anything he could to stop his hated nemesis from taking his job. He lobbied. He pouted. He froze out Young, and drove a wedge between his rival and his teammates. Amazed at some of Montana's displays was *San Francisco Chronicle* columnist C.W.

Nevius. "Can this really be Joe Cool," Nevius wrote "the guy who stood in there until fire-breathing blitzing linebackers were inches from his chest and then sailed a perfect spiral into the end zone? We kind of picture you as Clint Eastwood. Lately you are starting to sound like Don Knotts."

Young didn't deal with the whole "Joe-Steve" thing very well, either. He'd wake up in the morning, and have a difficult time getting out of bed, not wanting to make the drive to Santa Clara for practice. When he'd arrive in the parking lot of the 49er complex, the urge to turn around and drive away was always there. The cool responses he'd get from teammates weren't fun. The media hounded him about his and Montana's relationship, about the controversy. "Why go through this constant battle?" he'd ask himself. Young seriously thought about retiring to practice law full time. Imagine that, a guy who wanted to be a lawyer so he could get away from the pressure.

"I think there was so much going on at that time that was really overwhelming," says Paulshe Adcock, a close friend and confidante of Young's. "He was trying to deal with it little by little. There were a lot of great expectations from other people, and he was trying to step in and fill somebody's shoes that nobody wanted filled. I think he did the best he could do considering everything."

Realistically, Young couldn't quit. This was his chance. Everything was coming together for him just as it was unraveling for Montana. The 49ers were his team. Young survived the budding controversy between himself and Bono, rebounded from the so-so '91 campaign, and led San Francisco to a Montanaesque 14-2 mark. He led the league in passing for a third straight year, captured 56 of the 80 possible MVP votes cast by a nation-wide group of media members who covered the league, and won the Len Eshmont Award, given annually to the 49ers' most inspirational player. He was also the losing quarterback in the NFC Championship Game against the upstart Dallas Cowboys. Standing in the rain watching Joe Montana play one last time against the Detroit Lions was bad enough. But the loss to the Cowboys was a killer. Young thought they were going to win, and when they didn't, the Steve Young-haters were out in full force.

In that 1992 championship game, Young's statistics were strikingly similar to the Cowboys' Troy Aikman's. Young was 25 of 35 for 313 yards and a touchdown. Aikman was 24 of 34 for 322 yards and two touchdowns. The difference was the interceptions. Young had two; Aikman none. Dallas linebacker Ken Norton's interception of a Young pass in the fourth quarter was all the ammunition the Steve Young-can't-get-it-done-when-the-game's-on-the-line theorists needed. They'd forgotten about the bomb Young completed to Jerry Rice, called back by a Guy McIntyre holding penalty on the game's third play. They'd ignored the nine-play, 93-yard touchdown drive Young engineered on the series immediately following the Norton interception—all nine plays passes by the way. Also, nobody was blaming San Francisco cornerback Don Griffin, who allowed Alvin Harper to make a catch in front of him that turned into a 70-yard touchdown and sealed the deal.

Somebody had to be the fall guy. Why not Young? The lack of support by 49er fans for his client angered Young's agent Leigh Steinberg. He suggested Young look for another team. Young politely declined, saying San Francisco was where he wanted to be. It was not always clear why. Anywhere else and Young would have been worshipped. In San Francisco, he was a pariah. After the Dallas game, the phone calls to the sports talk shows were at their most ludicrous. "Joe would have seen Norton," or "Joe wouldn't have let himself get sacked by Charles Haley." Maybe the most ignominious attack of all was the scathing letter sent to Young signed "Mormons for Montana."

CHAPTER NINETEEN

A Legend Goes

Steve Young was in Provo, Utah, just another law student working on his JD. It wasn't so serene at 49er headquarters in Santa Clara. The place was like Vesuvius as an entire soap opera began playing out.

The Clash couldn't have sung it any better. "Should he stay or should he go?"

The "he" was Steve Young. The "he" was also Joe Montana. One was the 49ers' starting quarterback, the other used to be the 49ers' starting quarterback. And therein lay the problem. Joe Montana, who had lost his job to Steve Young, wasn't about to sit around in the twilight of his career and pull a Don Strock. Some quarterbacks were perfectly suited for the backup role. Joe Montana wasn't some quarterback.

After six seasons with two quarterbacks working in a less-than-peaceful coexistence, the top was ready to blow. Rumors were flying and teeth were gnashing in a city whose football fans were suffering a collective quarterback anxiety attack. Nobody knew what to believe.

First, Young was allegedly going to be traded to the Seattle Seahawks for two first-round picks that would allow the Niners to draft Notre Dame quarterback Rick

Mirer. That deal never materialized. New England apparently said no to a Young trade, as did—believe it or not—Tampa Bay. Then the spotlight landed on Montana, who had been shopping himself around the league since April 7. On April 16 things came to a head when Montana decided he wanted to play in Kansas City. The 49ers had given Montana permission to find a team and a deal, and he had done that. Everything was set until Edward DeBartolo Jr., Carmen Policy, George Seifert—take your pick—decided they didn't want to watch Montana ride off into the Missouri sunset. So they did what they had to do. They kicked the stool out from under Steve Young's feet. Fortunately, the noose wasn't yet around his neck.

In a bizarre twist to an equally bizarre saga, the San Francisco 49ers offered Montana his starting job back, and in the process, demoted the reigning league MVP, sending him to the bench. Nobody seemed to know if the proposal to Montana was legit or whether it was a public relations ploy. Seifert insisted it was his idea and his idea only. But Montana declined the chance to finish his career with the 49ers.

In Provo, Young laid low. It was better and easier that way. Once again, the franchise he loved had kicked him around. But Montana eventually did go to Kansas City, and Young, once and for all, was the starting quarterback. After treating Young like an ignored middle child, the 49ers finally decided to show their appreciation to their franchise player.

On July 15, a mere three months after the whole Montana affair had played itself out, the San Francisco 49ers awarded Young a five-year, $26 million-and-change contract that made him the highest paid player in

NFL history. Nine years had passed since the infamous $40 million contract Young had signed with the Express, and now he was making history again. This time around, Young was much more able to handle the publicity. Times had changed, but Young hadn't, at least not in the way he lived.

After bopping from place to place in the Bay Area—including a stint where he slept on a mattress on the floor in offensive lineman Harris Barton's house—Young arranged to move into a two-story structure in Los Altos Hills. The building was a performing arts studio. The first floor was used for dance classes for youngsters who ponied up big money to learn their craft. The second floor, what would become Young's home, was one big room with no bathroom or kitchen. When he moved in, he brought a couch, a bed, a television, a laser-disc player, and he filled his bookcases with books. He didn't bother to get a refrigerator or a lawn mower. The place came equipped with weeds, but no lawn. The landscaping would come later.

To eat, Young usually went to Draeger's, a high-end grocery store near his home featuring an elaborate deli. He also became a close personal friend of the Domino's Pizza delivery guy.

Conservative estimates say Young has $25 million in the bank.

"When he first came out to play for the 49ers, he was really afraid he was becoming this star and getting this money. He was really afraid of getting cocky and playing that role. So he was careful to keep himself humble. That kind of mentality caused him to not be excessive and not buy the most expensive car and live in the best house. That's what caused him to be frugal with his money. I've heard people say he's a miser. He's not like that at all. He definitely spends money where he thinks it's needed. He spends money on other people but not so much on himself," says a longtime friend.

One of the perils of living where he lives is that occasionally he's forced to listen to the tapping of little feet below him.

Young finds solace at home. It's the one place in the Bay Area where he isn't under a microscope.

Anywhere else and he has to deal with being the San Francisco 49ers' quarterback, which is what he had to do after another crushing loss to the Dallas Cowboys that financial security could not ameliorate. The Cowboys were better than the 49ers. They beat San Francisco in 1992 in the NFC Championship Game, they beat them in the 1993 regular season, and they beat them in the NFC Championship Game later that year. The quarterback of the second best team in football pulled up in front of his house and eased his aching body out of the car.

CHAPTER TWENTY

"Steve, Steve, Steve"

Some seasons things fall into place. The 1994 NFL season got off to a great start for Steve Young on April 22. At the Provo Tabernacle, Brigham Young University's J. Reuben Clark Law School held its commencement ceremonies. After six long, sometimes grueling semesters spread out over six long, sometimes grueling years, Young graduated from law school. When he first arrived at BYU in 1980, Young had designs on law school. He didn't know it would take 14 years for him to achieve that goal.

Before Young graduated, he told *San Francisco Chronicle* columnist Scott Ostler, "I actually feel that I struggle sometimes to find the real basic social value in being a quarterback. I see that I can do a lot more good with people as a lawyer than I can individually affect their lives throwing touchdowns or interceptions. My social conscience feels a lot better about being a lawyer."

Steve Young had to be the first guy in the history of the planet who used the words "social value" and "quarterback" in the same sentence. Yet with a juris doctorate in his possession, all he lacked was admittance from a state bar allowing him to practice law.

Well, that and a Super Bowl title as a starting quarterback.

As the NFL's 75th season began, most people saw the Dallas Cowboys and the San Francisco 49ers on a collision course once again.

Those close to the San Francisco 49ers looked at things a bit differently. In the season's second week, the Niners were scheduled to travel to Kansas City for a game with the Chiefs and You Know Who. Dallas would have to take a backseat for now. As much as Young wanted to treat the Kansas City game as one of 16 on the Niners' 1994 schedule, nobody else was going to do that. This was too good, too juicy. This was the one game when some 49er fans would root against San Francisco and cheer for Joe. The atmosphere prompted offensive guard Jesse Sapolu to say, "The bandwagon 49er fans jump off this week. They may love us but they love Joe even more. The true 49ers fans are behind us. All of us who played with Joe are fond of him, too. But that doesn't mean it wouldn't be great to beat him."

The whole thing was kind of spooky.

People figured Joe Montana would get his revenge, or Steve Young would prove the trading of Montana to be the correct move. In the game, the deck was stacked against Young. Playing behind a crippled offensive line, Young was a game participant. But when Sapolu went down with an injury in the first half, only one starter was left on the line and Young might as well have had a bullseye on his chest. He did his best before finally waving the white flag in the Chiefs' 24-17 victory. Young threw for more yardage, Montana threw two touchdowns. Young's completion percentage was better, but he also had two interceptions. And the 49ers lost the game. Young was battered, bruised, and diplomatic about the game Montana was savoring. Joe left Arrowhead Stadium holding the game ball.

As emotional and difficult as the Kansas City loss was for the 49ers, the season didn't really get going until week five against the Philadelphia Eagles. The Niners were cruising along at 3-1, feeling pretty good, especially after winning the Deion Sanders Sweepstakes. They signed the free agent cornerback extraordinaire to a one-year contract in mid-September. Free-agent acquisition Ken Norton, late of the Cowboys, was becoming more comfortable playing linebacker in San Francisco's system, and Steve Young was as potent as ever.

The Eagles came into Candlestick Park and it was a black day in the bay. They were a Ferrari to the Niners' 1965 Oldsmobile Dynamic. They outgained the 49ers, 437 yards to 189, and were making the game look amazingly simple. The banged-up Niner offensive line was totally ineffective, and the Eagle defense was teeing off on Young. When Philadelphia went ahead 33-8 in the third quarter, the seats in Candlestick Park began emptying. Too bad for those who left, because they missed a show they had never seen before and would probably never see again.

With 4:09 remaining in the third quarter, and the 49ers facing a third-and-10 situation, coach George Seifert had seen enough. After each hit to Young, Seifert winced. He couldn't afford to lose his quarterback, so he decided he wouldn't. Seifert sent backup Elvis Grbac into the game while Young's body parts were still attached. Grbac jogged onto the field, tapped Young on the shoulder, and told him he was done for the afternoon. Young couldn't believe it. He was livid. Why was he the only player being replaced? Was Seifert insinuating the loss was his fault? As Young made it to the sidelines, he lit into Seifert. With his helmet in hand, Young screamed at his coach and paced back and forth. A euphemism sometimes used by angry Mormons is "flippin' baloney." Young didn't use the euphemism.

Before the season, Young told friends he was going to be himself with the media. He had always been very careful about what he said, especially concerning Montana. Feeling like the 49ers were finally his team, Young decided to say what was on his mind and be more open with his feelings. In the first few weeks of the season, Young's plan hadn't worked. He seemed uncomfortable, even referring to Joe Montana as "the master" after the Kansas City game. It was as if he didn't want to offend Montana, even though Montana was nowhere to be found.

Young wanted to speak his mind more, but he didn't plan on an outburst like the one on the sideline on October 2. Yet for the first time since becoming a 49er, Young showed emotion that seemed genuine and real. His teammates noticed.

A group of Young's friends gathered in the players' lot after the game to wait for him. An hour passed and Young still hadn't emerged. After 90 minutes, offensive coordinator Mike Shanahan came out and said Young wouldn't be coming out for a while. That was the signal that there would be no party at Chili's. Stephanie Weston, Young's girlfriend, went into the locker room to console him. The rest of the group, almost on cue, dispersed.

Some called Young's sideline tirade the turning point in the 49ers' season. Others point to the following week in the Silverdome against the Detroit Lions. Still others say it was the Dallas game November 13. All three games proved to be crucial, but the Lion game seemed pivotal.

The 49ers laid an egg against Philadelphia, and nobody knew how the team would play on the road against an improved Detroit team a week later. When the Lions jumped to a quick 14-0 lead in the first quarter, the outlook was bleak. The Niner offensive line was still porous, Young was running for his life, and one wire-service photo seemed to say it all. The picture showed Young after a particularly brutal hit. He was on the Silverdome carpet looking like a GI along the Ho Chi Minh Trail, in a prone position with a helpless look on his face. Not long after that photo was taken, the comeback began. San Francisco tied things by halftime and ended up with a 27-21 win. In the first quarter a 3-3 record looked realistic, but the 49ers left Michigan 4-2. They wouldn't lose for another 77 days.

The following week against Atlanta, Young was brilliant. He was perfect on his first 14 passes, and only had one incompletion all day (15 of 16 overall) in the 42-3 win. A week later against Tampa Bay, a funny thing happened. Young had always had to listen to a smattering of boos when his name was announced before a home game. But in the first home game since the Philadelphia debacle, Young heard nothing but cheers as public address announcer Joe Starkey said "Steve Young." There were a few more fans wearing Steve Young replica jerseys too. It had been seven years in coming, but Young appeared to finally be winning over the 49er faithful.

The next demon to exorcise was the Dallas Cowboys. The midseason game was billed as an NFC Championship

Game preview, and San Francisco beat the Cowboys 21-14. The win sewed up home-field advantage for the 49ers, something they desperately wanted should they have to face Dallas again. Every player felt sure they would see the Cowboys again.

The Dallas-San Francisco rematch came on January 15, and the revenge was sweet. Three Dallas turnovers in the game's early minutes gave San Francisco an insurmountable 21-0 lead. The crowd was going bonkers and so was Young. He had only felt joy like this on the football field two other times, and both came at BYU. For the first time as a professional football player he was euphoric. He wasn't just going to the Super Bowl like he had done twice previously, he was taking the team with him. On his back.

When Young met Dallas quarterback Troy Aikman at midfield following the 38-28 win, Aikman said, "It's your year." Aikman was passing the torch. He'd had two years of glory and now it was Young's turn.

The quarterback who had worked for so long for this chance, who had stood on the sidelines as Joe Montana led the 49ers to so many key wins, had finally done it himself. After shaking Aikman's hand, Young took off on a victory lap around the stadium, a display as spontaneous as his victory dance in the Holiday Bowl his senior year. As Young ran, the crowd chanted, "Steve. Steve. Steve." As the adrenaline flowed, Young unintentionally knocked over several cameramen and photographers who had gotten in his way. As he continued running, the chant changed to "MVP. MVP. MVP."

The entire scene was amazing. Young had completed 13 of 29 passes for 155 yards, less than half the yardage he had thrown for in the first NFC Championship Game loss to Dallas in the 1992 season. His completion percentage was only 44 percent. But as Young learned so many years earlier at BYU in the game against UCLA when he was outplayed by Steve Bono, to the winner goes the spoils.

Steve Young had gone to the Super Bowl on two other occasions. Both times, it was as a backup. During the media day crush, when players are asked seemingly every conceivable question—even some about football—Young would watch as the stars of the team, Joe Montana, Jerry Rice, Roger Craig, and Ronnie Lott, would garner most of the attention. As the backup quarterback, Young drew little notice. And when he did, most of the questions centered on his status playing behind a living, breathing legend. How did he stay patient? Would he remain a 49er? Was it frustrating riding the bench? Despite being miserable, Young would diplomatically answer each question, masking how he really felt. He was glad to be at the Super Bowl, he'd say. He only wished the circumstances were different.

In 1995, they were.

The questions the media horde asked Young days before Super Bowl XXIX as the 49ers prepared for their game with the San Diego Chargers were the same questions Montana used to field. Young was the centerpiece now, the superstar everybody wanted to talk to. Elvis Grbac had assumed the role Young was so acquainted with. Instead of "Steve, what's it like playing behind such a great quarterback?" the questions began, "Elvis, what's it like . . ."

• • •

At the 1980 Winter Olympics when the United States hockey team won the gold medal, the pivotal game in the Americans' run for the gold was their 4-3 "Do you believe in miracles?" upset win over the Soviet Union. What many people fail to remember is all the win over the Russians did was vault the U.S. into the gold-medal game against Finland, which the U.S. won, 4-2. The 1994 San Francisco 49ers' situation was not unlike the 1980 United States hockey team's.

The Niners had beaten the Dallas Cowboys in the NFC Championship Game to get to the Super Bowl. They still had some work to do. Beating the Cowboys was not enough. They needed one more win, and it was the San Diego Chargers who stood between San Francisco and the gold medal.

The Chargers' chances of beating the 49ers were roughly the same as a pre-game snowstorm in Miami's Joe Robbie Stadium. Yet there was still the longer-than-long shot chance San Diego could pull off the upset. San Francisco was having none of that.

The Chargers were the AFC's sacrificial lamb in Super Bowl XXIX, and they barely put up a fight.

Steve Young was the main reason. One minute and 24 seconds into the game, San Francisco led 7-0. On San Francisco's third offensive play after receiving the kick-off, Jerry Rice, split wide to the right, ran toward the middle of the field, cut between safeties Stanley Richard and Darren Carrington and cradled in a perfect pass from Young at the San Diego 15-yard-line. The future hall-of-famer sauntered in from there and another in a long line of Super Bowl routs was on. The Niners took a 14-0 lead with 11:05 left in the first quarter when Young found Ricky Watters for a 51-yard hookup. By halftime, San Francisco had completely worked San Diego. The Niners led 28-10, Young had completed 17 of 23 passes for 239 yards and four touchdowns, and Most Valuable Player ballots with Young's name on them were already being cast.

Young's fifth TD toss was a 15-yarder to Jerry Rice in the third quarter. With 13:49 left in the game, Young found Rice again for his sixth touchdown pass. Six touchdown passes broke the Super Bowl record of five, set by none other than Joe Montana.

The Cult of Montana, the so-called "Branch Montanians," that loud, fractious group still solidly behind the four-time Super Bowl winner, had to sit down and shut up. For the three previous years, Young had the NFL's top quarterback rating. Nobody in the grand history of the league had ever done that. He led the NFL again in 1994, and this time Young's detractors couldn't refer to Young as a guy who piled up impressive stats with nothing to show for it. Young's six-TD Super Bowl performance took care of that argument. They said the only reason Young succeeded was because of the 49ers' system and because of Jerry Rice, conveniently forgetting that Joe Montana played in the 49ers' system throwing to Jerry Rice. They said Young could never replace Montana. They were wrong.

At the conclusion of Super Bowl XXIX, Young, who learned he was the game's MVP, deviated from the normal course. He wasn't going to take all the glory himself.

At Super Bowl XXIII, even though Jerry Rice was named MVP, it was Joe Montana who filmed the "I'm going to Disneyland" commercial immediately following the game. Before Super Bowl XXIX, Young and Rice decided that should either one be named the game's MVP, they would utter the famous lines together.

So they did.

In the ensuing press conference, Young spoke about what being the winning quarterback in a Super Bowl meant, especially considering everything he'd endured to get to this point. "It's a spectacular feeling. There were many days a few years ago when I'd get to work and I'd almost want to turn around. Honestly, it was difficult for one person to face the kind of scrutiny and skepticism and tough times. As I look back at that, it was one of the most precious times in my life that I could play through that and stand here today."

The emotion of the moment was beginning to show.

In the locker room, cameramen, photographers, and reporters jostled for space and for people to talk to. Martin Wyatt of San Francisco's KGO took Young aside and began interviewing the Super Bowl MVP. Wyatt began the interview and then gave way to Young, who was choking back tears.

"To the fans in the Bay Area, I understood all along. There were days when I was driving to work and I'd turn the corner and say, 'Maybe I'll go home.' But I wouldn't. Honestly, there were some tough moments. But I just kept showing up at work."

At that point, Young excused himself. It was an emotionally charged moment, very similar to the one he had experienced in Cougar Stadium following his final home game as a BYU Cougar, the last time he'd thrown six touchdown passes in a game.

When the *New York Daily News* asked Young about his six-touchdown feat, he was incredulous. "I wouldn't have believed it if I wrote it down. Six touchdowns, it's impossible. I've played football for 25 years and four is the most I ever threw."

Six touchdown passes didn't come often, but Young proved he knew how to pick his spots when they did, even if he couldn't remember the other time.

As the revelry continued, Young tried to soak it all in. Just as Montana clutched the ball after the September victory over the 49ers, Young did the same thing in the Joe Robbie Stadium locker room in the aftermath of Super Bowl XXIX. Only the ball Steve Young held was silver, and it had a name, The Vince Lombardi Trophy.

CHAPTER TWENTY-ONE

It's A Wonderful Life

A t the Steve Young Charity Auction on May 20, 1995, at the San Francisco Hilton Hotel, it was clear the San Francisco 49er quarterback and eponymous host of the event had not allowed the past season's achievements to change him. The two-time league MVP, the Super Bowl MVP, and the quarterback who threw six touchdown passes against the San Diego Chargers in the Super Bowl came to his own Forever Young Foundation event—a black-tie–optional affair—a bit under dressed. Young, the master of ceremonies, was wearing a tan suit. No explanation was necessary. It was his gig, and he wasn't about to put on a tuxedo. Auction organizers were just happy he wasn't sporting untied tennis shoes.

The man on top of the professional football world is still the same guy he's always been. He lives in a dorm-like room in California during the football season and in a 106-year-old pioneer farm house in Utah when he's not playing football. He traded in the Buick he won for being selected Super Bowl MVP for a Dodge pickup. His is a relatively simple life, made much easier now that he's gotten rid of the Super Bowl stigma that dogged him for so long. So what can he possibly do for an encore?

Young entered the 1995 NFL season shooting for his fifth consecutive league passing title. He was also coming off one of the greatest—if not the greatest—season an NFL quarterback has ever enjoyed. In 1994, Young completed 70 percent of his passes, threw for 3,969 yards, and 35 touchdowns. His 112.8 quarterback rating broke Joe Montana's single season mark, and Young's numbers were actually modest. Because the Niners were so dominant, especially in the latter part of the season, Young rarely played an entire game, often viewing the waning moments of a blowout standing on the sidelines wearing a baseball cap. Imagine what his stats would have looked like if the games had been close and he was throwing the ball in the fourth quarter.

Those things hardly mattered. Young only wanted to win a championship, and he achieved that goal. Now he's venturing into uncharted waters.

Now Young wonders what's left for him to accomplish. He's constantly said he still has the competitive drive and that the fire isn't gone. When he showed up for the 49ers' training camp in Rocklin, California, in July, he publicly admitted he was excited to begin another season. He even proved it by reporting to camp with the rookies and free agents, three days before he was required to be there. Privately, though, his attitude wasn't so buoyant. Young admitted to friends that the Super Bowl victory had eliminated much of the sense of urgency he always felt. He even allowed that despite the difficulties associated with the pressures of being the 49ers' quarterback, it was almost better before he won the Super Bowl because there was always something for him to chase, some other mountain to climb.

"You work so many years to get to here, and you never give a thought to what you do when you do it," Young said during the off-season. "It's been a weird experience. I was insane trying to get to the Super Bowl. It's been such a focus for so long. You use it as an incentive for so long and then all of a sudden it's gone. The things you used over the years to motivate you are accomplished."

The Denver Broncos' John Elway and Dan Marino of the Miami Dolphins, the two best quarterbacks in the NFL without a ring, are now the ones chasing the elusive Super Bowl victory. While they stand in the shoes Young was in one season ago, Young is shooting for a second consecutive championship.

"I think the thing about Steve is he won't be satisfied now that he's won the Super Bowl," says a close friend. "He's the type who will say, 'I've won one, so let's win another, and then another.' He definitely won't be satisfied."

Young may lead the Niners to another title—the Niners are still loaded and Young is in his prime—but he will probably have trouble replicating the drama of the remarkable 1994 season. What is the next thing, the next challenge? Another passing title? Another MVP season? They're certainly all within his grasp, as is the Pro Football Hall of Fame.

The one thing Young does recognize is how different 1995 will be. For the first time since childhood, Young sees it as a chance to play football not for the money, not for the glory, not for the trophies, and not for the championships. Young envisions his post-Super Bowl season as a chance to play football as a pro for the very same reason he began playing football on his front lawn in Salt Lake City as a kid. To Young, football is supposed to be fun.

"I see myself playing football this year for the pure love I have for the game. It's why I've been playing for 25 years. It's a fun game. It should be a fun game," he says.

The two boys would finish their homework and immediately grab a football. The Young boys, Steve and Mike, exactly two years apart in age, would go outside their home in Connecticut and either toss the football in their yard, or walk down the street to North Mianus Elementary School and begin their games of pretend. It was a simple deal, really. Steve and Mike were in the Super Bowl. They were in an impossible situation—they were a touchdown behind and time was running out. Yet in the game's final minute, with seemingly no chance to win, a tight spiral from Steve would make it through the imaginary defender's hands and into Mike's waiting arms. The celebration began as the two brothers imagined the noise of the crowd celebrating the game-winning touchdown. They were Super Bowl champs. The best in the world.

Then they'd go home because Mom had dinner ready.

Only now does Steve Young understand that those imaginary games he used to play in Greenwich with his brother don't even come close to comparing to the real thing.

Index

INDEX